The Best of
Guideposts®

The Best of
Guideposts.

A COLLECTION OF STORIES
FROM AMERICA'S FAVORITE MAGAZINE

Ideals Publications
Nashville, Tennessee

ISBN 0-8249-4640-5

Published by Ideals Publications
A division of Guideposts
535 Metroplex Drive, Suite 250
Nashville, Tennessee 37211
www.idealsbooks.com

Publisher, Patricia A. Pingry
Editor, Peggy Schaefer
Designer, Marisa Calvin
Copy Editors, Marie Brown, Melinda Rathjen
Cover photograph, David Noton Photography/Alamy

Library of Congress Cataloging-in-Publication Data

The best of Guideposts : a collection of stories from America's favorite magazine.
    p. cm.
  Includes index.
  ISBN 0-8249-4640-5 (alk. paper)
  1. Christian life. I. Guideposts (Pawling, N.Y.)
  BV4515.3.B47 2005
  242—dc22
                                    2004023222

Printed and bound in Italy

10 9 8 7 6 5 4 3 2 1

ACKNOWLEDGMENTS
All stories in this book are taken from *Guideposts* magazine,
copyright © Guideposts, Carmel, New York 10512.

* When Mediamark Research Inc. asked readers of 206 major magazines to name
their favorites, *Guideposts* ranked number one among adults and women in their
spring 2004 study.

Contents

Foreword

BEFORE THE WORLD WIDE WEB, before chatrooms and online bulletin boards, before the interconnectedness of the global Internet community, there was *Guideposts*.

For more than sixty years, since Norman Vincent Peale (the man who would go on to write that granddaddy of all self-help books, *The Power of Positive Thinking*) founded *Guideposts*, the magazine has built its reputation on the strength of a community of readers who tell their stories in its pages—true stories of hope and inspiration. In today's cyber-jargon, that's called "user-generated content." In Peale's day, it was simply known as storytelling.

The book you have in your hands contains our very best stories, the ones that have continued to make *Guideposts* magazine America's favorite source of inspiration. These stories are told in a compelling first-person style that puts you inside the narrator's life and in touch with the narrator's emotions, whether the author is a celebrity or an everyday person. You'll hear from truck drivers and celebrated writers, stay-at-home moms and CEOs, war heroes and schoolteachers. You'll meet a postal worker who survived deadly anthrax poisoning, a father who lost a daughter in the Oklahoma

City bombing and forgave her killers, a woman who talked an escaped convict into surrendering while he held her hostage in her own home, a grandmother reunited with a grandson after decades of separation, and a beloved ballplayer and TV announcer who recalls his favorite Christmas gift from his hardscrabble childhood. From major, life-changing events to quiet, unexpected moments of grace, each story will enrich your faith and inspire you to better living.

You'll read another kind of story too—"His Mysterious Ways," our most popular column for more than twenty years. Here are those true and unforgettable occurrences that defy rational explanation: the phone call at just the right moment, a stranger who inexplicably appears to save the day, a dream that is more than a dream, a mysterious voice beckoning us to safety. These experiences send chills down our spines and grant us a magnificent glimpse of something beyond the world of our daily lives, the work of a power greater than ourselves. *Much greater.*

This collection will move you, inspire you, and give you the kind of hope and encouragement countless millions of readers have found in *Guideposts*. Why has *Guideposts* been so extraordinarily successful through six decades as the world's greatest inspirational magazine? True, our interfaith publication talks of God and faith and the indomitable power of the human spirit. Yet the secret to *Guideposts* is that it is about people—written by real people, like you, who meet their struggles and challenges with an optimism and enthusiasm that lifts them above life's rough spots.

So get ready for some real "user-generated content," and some *great* storytelling.

—EDWARD GRINNAN, Editor-in-Chief, *Guideposts*

The Power of Prayer

I Believe in Prayer

Captain Eddie Rickenbacker

February 1945

There are a lot of things concerning the human mind and soul that we don't know much about. We get glimpses of them when, in times of danger or suffering, we cross a little way over the line of ordinary thought.

As I roared down the last stretch in an automobile race years ago, I felt that I could control that machine with my mind, that I could hold it together with my mind, and that, if it finally collapsed, I could run it with my mind.

If I had said such a thing then, the boys would have called me crazy. Even now I can't explain it. But I believe that if you think disaster, you will get it. Brood about death, and you hasten your demise. Think with confidence and faith, and life becomes more secure, more fraught with action, richer in achievement.

Perhaps such things as the control of mind over matter and the transmission of thought waves are tied up together, part of something so big we haven't grasped it yet. It's part of us and part of the

Something that is looking after us. It's one of the things that makes me believe in personal protection and in life after death. I have difficulty putting it into words.

A strange thing happened to me some years ago. I was flying to Chicago. It was in the middle of December, and the weather was miserable. There was a lot of ice. We suddenly lost the radio beam. For a long time we cruised back and forth trying to pick it up. Fog was all around us. We were lost, off the beam, and flying blind. Our two-way radio went out, and we had lost all communication with the world. For seven hours we flew—where, we didn't know.

Darkness was coming on. Then, suddenly, we saw a break in the murk. The pilot brought the ship down to within one hundred feet of land, and we saw lights flashing by on a four-lane highway. We followed it for some distance.

Then we saw a red glow away off to the right, headed for it, and saw a river gleaming. We flew up that river, and out of the six-thirty dusk of winter, I saw the Toledo-Edison sign flashing. Skimming the roofs, we circled and landed at the airport. We had just enough gas left for eleven minutes of flight.

We had flown blind, without a beam, but we were on a beam, just the same. I like to think it was the "Big Radio" that kept us going—the Thing that keeps all of us flying safely through the fog and night, toward some mysterious and important goal. The "Big Radio" is a two-way job. You've got to keep tuned with It, and you have to talk back. I believe in prayer. I learned to pray as a kid at my mother's knee.

One day in France, during World War I, with only one magneto on my Newport biplane functioning, I was attacked by three

German Albatross planes. I came out of a dive so fast that the terrific pressure collapsed my right-hand upper wing. No matter what I tried, I couldn't come out of that whirl of death. I often wish I could think as fast under normal conditions as I did during that drop. While I fought the controls and tried to get the engine going, I prayed, "Oh, God, help me get out of this."

As a last desperate act, I threw my weight to the left side over the cockpit and jammed the controls, then jammed the engine wide open. The thing suddenly sputtered and vibrated violently, and the plane sailed away on her one good wing for France. I held it like that all the way home.

This escape and others I have had were not the result of any super ability or super knowledge on my part. I wouldn't be alive if I had to depend on that. I realized then, as I headed for France on one wing, that there had to be Something else. I had seen others die—men brighter and more able than I. I knew there was a Power. I believe in calling upon it for help.

I am not such an egotist as to believe that God has spared me because I am I. I believe there is work for me to do and I am spared to do it, just as you are. If I die tomorrow, I do not fear the prospect at all.

On a rainy night in February 1941, I had the worst accident of my life. As I look back on the agonizing days in the hospital that followed, I realize there was a reason behind it all. It was a test and a preparation for what was to follow.

In the four months I lay in that hospital, I did more thinking about life and death than I had ever done before. Twenty-one months later I was adrift in an open lifeboat with seven other starving men, most of them so young they needed the strength and understanding of a man who had been down in the valley of the shadow, who had suffered and made sense out of his suffering. To those men I was able to bring the distilled essence of the religious philosophy I had developed while in the hospital.

Once while hospitalized I almost died from a throat hemorrhage. "Here," I said, "is death."

Then it dawned upon me in a flash that the easiest thing in the world is to die; the hardest is to live. Dying was a sensuous pleasure; living was a grim task. In that moment I chose to live. I knew from experience that abandonment to death was a sin. I wasn't quitting. I had work to do, others to serve.

Many other things came to me as well. I realized I wasn't afraid to die, because I had lived so much, in good ways and bad, that I no longer felt the youthful pang of not having lived at all. I knew only the sorrow of being unable to help other people anymore. And when I finally came around, I saw life and death and the meaning of the Golden Rule more clearly than I had ever known.

I had taken that clarity with me to the rubber raft in the South Pacific after our plane crashed. Throughout those twenty-one days of blistering sun and nights of ghastly chill, I never lost faith, and I felt that we were adrift for a purpose. I saw that life had no meaning except in terms of helping others.

I think man does not instinctively interest himself in others. He does it only by an act of will, when he sees that "I am my brother's keeper" and "Do unto others" are the essence of all truth.

My experiences and the suffering through which I passed have taught me that faith in God is the answer to life.

Ten Men and a Prayer

FRED SCHILLER

May 1952

I was a buck private attached to Company C of the 846 Signal Photo Battalion. Sitting next to me in the station waiting room was a lieutenant of the much-decorated Third Infantry Division just back from European combat. It was early 1945.

When we started casual talk, I discovered that his name was McBride and that he was going home to Indiana on furlough. He told of one experience with moving simplicity, then left to catch his train. His story is still so vivid in my mind, even after seven years, that I have an almost irresistible compulsion to relate it. . . .

Italian hill "46" was finally abandoned on orders one bleak spring day back in 1944. As the weary GIs filed back towards the little Italian town of San Pietro, behind which American artillery answered the enemy, Sergeant Frazer began counting the human cost of their mission.

"How many men left in your squad, Murphy?"

"Four, counting myself."

Frazer then moved down the thin line of troops towards Max Halpern, a grizzled, flint-eyed corporal, who carried a light machine gun cradled in his arm like a baby.

"Rosy got his right after the jump," said the corporal. "Best squad leader I ever had." "Rosy" was Sergeant Rosenberg.

The remnants of the platoon then moved into the shattered village. The rest of their company had gathered beside a small church with only three walls and half a roof left. The section leaders were conferring with Lieutenant McBride beside the torn wall of the church.

"We'll wait here till the battalion assembles," said the officer. "Have your men ready to move out again in half an hour."

Corporal Halpern signaled his men to relax and, still cradling the machine gun, walked into the cool shadows inside the church. He didn't want to talk to anybody just then; he was feeling too keenly about his buddy "Rosy," who had touched off the mine explosion that had cleared the way for the rest of the squad's advance.

Halpern looked wearily around the quiet, littered pews. Amazingly, the cross above the altar remained in place; and in the aisle, in front of the pews, knocked from its pedestal by the concussion of shell fire but still upright, stood a statue of Christ. Glass and plaster fragments were everywhere, even on the altar and chancel floor.

For the first time in three days, the knots inside Halpern began to loosen. He realized how tired he was. And the loss of a buddy overwhelmed him. Corporal Halpern lifted his eyes toward the altar and the sky above the shattered roof.

Oh, God, he thought, *why—*

Suddenly Halpern laid his machine gun in a corner and walked outside to Lieutenant McBride.

"Lieutenant, while we're waiting, I want to round up ten fellows of our faith and say a prayer for Sergeant Rosenberg."

"Sure, Corporal. But why ten?"

"It's the Jewish prayer, 'Minjeh.' According to Hebrew ritual it requires ten Hebrews."

The corporal went off up the street among the rubble heaps and the little groups of men. When he returned, some minutes later, with a group of fellow GIs, the lieutenant was standing inside the church.

"Found them okay, Corporal?"

"No," said Halpern, "I'm short one man. Been through the whole battalion, but the rest are either killed or wounded. Don't know what I can do without the tenth either." The corporal looked from his friends to the lieutenant.

"I don't think the Almighty would mind too much if one were absent," said Lieutenant McBride.

Corporal Halpern glanced toward the altar of the church and then up through the torn roof.

"I'll manage, Lieutenant," he said. "Come on, fellows." The corporal led the way down the church aisle and in silence arranged the eight men and himself in a circle before the chancel.

The lieutenant, at the back of the church, uncovered his head in reverence and then looked in surprise as he saw what Halpern was doing.

The corporal gently lifted the statue of Christ and placed it in the circle between two of his buddies.

"Jesus was a Jew," he said softly. "He makes us ten."

Then he took out a little prayer book. "Repeat after me," he said to the quiet circle of his Jewish comrades. The prayer of "Minjeh" rose solemnly. . . . Sergeant Rosenberg would not be forgotten.

The Girl Who Was Frozen Solid

JEAN HILLIARD VIG

February 1984

I grabbed my purse and the car keys, threw on my new green, waist-length parka, and started toward the door. Mom called, "Jean, aren't you going to take your boots and snowmobile pants? It's supposed to get colder tonight."

I'd lived on a farm in northern Minnesota all my life and was used to cold weather. "I'll be fine, Mom. I'm just driving into town to meet some friends. It's not that cold."

I was nineteen years old and thought cowboy boots and blue jeans were more appropriate than warm clothing for a night out with friends. Besides, I had no idea that in just a few hours the temperature would plummet to twenty-five degrees below zero with gusts of fifty-mile-an-hour blizzard winds.

Around midnight, after a fun evening in Fosston with my friends, I was driving home in Dad's big white Ford LTD. I usually took the four-wheel-drive pickup, but tonight it was low on gas and Dad had said I could take the car.

As I was heading home, the snow sparkled festively in the beams of my headlights. I decided to take the old country gravel road because it was a few miles shorter than the blacktop. Besides, I had always loved that road. It meandered through a forest of tall pines. Every couple of miles a house or a farm dotted the landscape, but the rest was pure picture-postcard scenery—icy-blue Minnesota lakes, tall trees, and the narrow, winding, hilly gravel road.

I didn't see the small patch of ice in the middle of the road because of the new snow. Before I knew what was happening, the car skidded off to the side and the front wheel slid precariously close to the ditch. I tried to back up slowly, but the tires were spinning. When I put the car in forward gear, the front tire slipped off the shoulder and the car became helplessly marooned.

I wasn't frightened, but I sure was disgusted! I could just hear Dad's booming voice when he found out what I'd done with his good car.

I knew there was a house a half mile or so ahead, so I got out of the car, slammed the door, and stomped off down the road, forgetting my hat on the front seat.

I was steaming over the mess I had gotten myself into, and my anger kept me warm for a few hundred feet. The wind forced me to zip up my jacket collar over my nose and mouth. I shoved my hands deep into my pockets and dug into the snow in my pointy-toed leather cowboy boots.

I walked on a little farther and then remembered Wally's place, in the opposite direction. *It should be just a half mile or so,* I thought. Wally was an acquaintance of my folks and I knew he had a four-wheel-drive truck that could easily pull my car out of the ditch.

As I passed the car, I felt like kicking the tire, but I trudged on. After a half mile or so, I passed a house. It was dark and there were no tracks in the driveway. *Probably out of town,* I thought.

I struggled up another hill. Finally, I thought I saw Wally's farm in the distance. *Yes!* There was the long lane leading to his house. I was breathing harder. And then . . . I blanked out.

Although I don't remember it, apparently I half-walked, half-stumbled, falling at times, down that long lane. I crawled the last hundred feet or so on my hands and knees, but I don't remember doing that either.

By now, the wind-chill factor was seventy to eighty degrees below zero. Right at Wally's front door I collapsed and fell face forward into the snow. And that's where I lay all night.

The next morning Wally came out his front door just before seven o'clock. Normally he didn't go to work until eight, but, thank God, he decided to go in early that morning. Wally saw my body in the snow; he leaned down and tried to find a pulse. There was none. My swollen face was a gray, ashen color. My eyes were frozen open. I wasn't breathing.

Wally still doesn't know how he managed to pick me up and get me into his car. He said it was like struggling with a 120-pound cordwood stick or a big piece of meat out of the freezer.

At the hospital in Fosston, Wally yelled through the emergency room doorway for help. He picked me up under my arms and a couple of nurses lifted my ankles. My body didn't bend anywhere.

As they were putting me on a stretcher, one nurse exclaimed, "She's frozen solid!" Another nurse, the mother of one of my best friends, said, "I think it's Jean Hilliard! I recognize her blond hair and the green jacket!"

Mrs. Rosie Erickson, who works in bookkeeping, ran out in the hall when she heard the commotion. She leaned over my body. "Wait! Listen!" A hush fell around my stretcher. "It's a moaning sound . . . coming from her throat! Listen!"

I was wheeled into the emergency room. Dr. George Sather, our family doctor, was on duty that morning. He was unable to hear any breathing or a heartbeat with his stethoscope. Then he attached a heart monitor, which picked up a very slow, faint heartbeat. A cardiologist said it seemed to be "a dying heart."

"We have to get these boots off!" Dr. Sather exclaimed. "Bring some blankets! She's still alive!" The emergency room sprang to life. My boots and jacket were the only clothing items they could get off immediately. The rest of my clothes were frozen on me.

When they cut my jeans off, the staff saw that my feet were black, and there were black areas on my legs and lower back. My feet and legs were swollen. The tissue damage seemed so severe that when my parents arrived, Dr. Sather told them that if I did live, my legs might have to be amputated. He wanted my parents to be prepared.

Dr. Sather ordered oxygen, and a nurse suggested trying Aqua-K pads. Just the day before, a new kind of water-filled heating pad had arrived at the hospital. Quickly the nurses unpacked one heating-pad box after another. Fortunately, the only nurse on the staff who knew how to connect them to the special water-filled machines was on duty, and she directed the operation.

My body was frozen so solid that they couldn't pierce my skin with a hypodermic needle. There was no way at first to give me any medication to speed the thawing process or to prevent infection. But the medical team didn't know what Rosie Erickson was about to do.

Rosie found my parents in the hall. "Mr. and Mrs. Hilliard, do you mind if I put Jean on the prayer chain at our church?"

Mom, who was completely bewildered at the scene before her, answered quickly, "Yes . . . please do!"

Mrs. Erickson hurried to her office and made a phone call to the prayer chain chairman at the Baptist church where her husband is pastor. The prayer chain was set in motion. The first person on the list called the second. That person called the third and so on.

My heart started beating slightly faster. Even though still far slower than the normal rate of about seventy-two beats a minute, the doctors were overjoyed. Slowly I started breathing on my own.

The prayer chain was lengthening. Mrs. Erickson called the pastors of the Lutheran, Catholic, Methodist, and Bethel Assembly churches in Fosston. They, in turn, called the chairmen of their prayer chain groups, who passed the word along.

During the first hours that the prayer chain was underway, my legs and feet, instead of getting darker as Dr. Sather expected, started to lighten and regain their natural color. One after another, the doctors and nurses filed in to marvel at the pinkish tinge appearing at the line on my upper thighs where Dr. Sather had thought they might have to amputate.

The prayer chain spread to the nearby towns of Crookston and Bemidji, and Grand Forks, North Dakota. Soon hundreds, then thousands of people were aware that a young woman had been brought in to the Fosston hospital frozen solid and was in desperate need of God's miraculous healing.

One of the nurses, on her way to get more blankets, poked her head into Mrs. Erickson's doorway and said, "She might make it! Her legs are starting to regain color at the top! And her heart is beating stronger!"

Mrs. Erickson looked up at the clock and thought, *The prayer chain is in full swing now. God is answering those prayers already. Of course she's going to make it!*

At that moment the whole attitude in my hospital room changed. Now, instead of "She probably won't survive," the feeling was "Perhaps she'll live, but she will surely lose her legs from the knees down."

Before noon that day I stirred and moaned a word that sounded like "Mom." My mother and oldest sister Sandra stayed near my bed, holding, squeezing, and patting my hands. "Jean, Jean, wake up! Jeannie, can you hear me? It's Mom. Sandra's here too. Jeannie, we love you. Jeannie, can you hear?" Around noon I mumbled a few words to them.

All over the area the prayer chain continued.

By mid-afternoon I woke up and started thrashing in bed. The doctors told me later that I moaned and yelled so much that they were convinced I would have severe brain damage.

All day the nurses and doctors watched in amazement as the blackness in my legs and feet disappeared inch by inch.

By late afternoon Dr. Sather thought perhaps my legs would be saved and that only my feet might have to be amputated. A few hours later he was astounded to realize that perhaps it would be just my toes.

In the end I did not lose any part of my body! Normal color and circulation came back to even the blackest parts of my legs, feet, and toes.

Dr. Sather had also thought he would have to do numerous skin grafts where huge blisters covered my toes. But these places healed too without skin grafting.

Indeed, after watching my body become whole again, I am convinced that a miracle occurred. Even Dr. Sather said, "I just took care of her. God healed her."

The doctors kept me in the hospital seven weeks to make sure of my recovery from frostbite and to lessen the possibility of any infection in my toes. And that entire time I never once experienced any fear. I'm convinced it was the prayer chain that kept me calm and filled me with a positive faith that I would be healed.

The night I nearly froze to death was over three years ago—December 20, 1980. Since then I have met a wonderful man, got married, had a beautiful baby girl, and am expecting our second child. My husband, my daughter, and I live on a farm outside Fosston, and my life is a tranquil, happy one. But there isn't a day that goes by that I don't think about the night I nearly froze to death.

I've become a different person because of that experience. Last winter I joined forces with a civil defense expert, an army sergeant, a highway patrolman, and a doctor from Crookston who is an expert in hypothermia. We give talks about winter survival to people in neighboring towns and counties. I tell them my story and point out what can happen when people go out in the winter unprepared for the weather.

I'm surprised I can do this, because when I was in high school, I was absolutely terrified of speech class. The thought of standing in front of people with all eyes on me almost made me sick to my stomach. But now I feel none of that. I'm proud to share my story with the hope that I can help even one person avoid the mistakes I made.

I believe this is the reason God spared me—so that I can help other people learn how to survive the changeable and very cold winters.

I've changed in other ways too. My family and I are much closer now. I appreciate every day I'm alive, and I have an enormous respect for the power of prayer. I believe that the prayer chains saved my life. Thousands of people I didn't even know bombarded heaven with powerful prayer requests in my behalf, and against all medical odds I survived. I not only lived, I survived as a completely normal, whole human being without needing even so much as a skin graft. In fact, unlike most other people who have suffered from frostbite, I don't experience any ill effects from the cold.

As one minister reminded me in the hospital when we spoke of the prayer chain, we as God's children have been commanded to "Pray without ceasing" (1 Thessalonians 5:17).

And I'm sure that was what created my miracle—all those people praying unceasingly for me.

His Mysterious Ways

THE DREAM was so vivid and unusual that I told my husband about it as soon as I awoke. "I was explaining to a woman with shoulder-length, golden-brown hair and a white lab coat that I felt a pain in my left breast," I said. "But I've never noticed anything like that."

"You should see your gynecologist, just in case," he said. I did and, to my shock, there was a lump in my breast. When the results of my biopsy came in, the doctor informed me I had a cancerous tumor. He wanted to perform a mastectomy.

"Couldn't you do a more conservative surgery?" I asked. "Take out just the lump?"

"No," he replied. "A mastectomy is the best course of treatment."

"I'd like a second opinion," I said. He referred me to another specialist. But that doctor's brusque manner left me cold.

A friend then gave me the name of her oncologist. Before my appointment, I did all the reading I could on breast cancer so I'd be able to make a more informed decision about surgery and treatment. The most important thing, though, would be finding a doctor I could trust. *Lord,* I asked, *how will I know who's the right one for me?*

My friend's oncologist put me at ease right away, and I told him I wanted to avoid losing my breast, if at all possible. "I'd like you to see this surgeon I work with," he said, then set up an appointment for me.

I drove straight over. The moment I saw the surgeon, I knew that I'd finally found my doctor. Standing there in her white lab coat, her honey-colored hair falling around her shoulders, was the woman I'd seen in my dream.

—ANNE ABRUZZINI, *April 2000*

The Miracle Day

BARBARA CUMMISKEY

April 1985

I still remember the whispers as I struggled through the halls in high school. "Look at her stagger!" I'd hear them say. "I'll bet she's drunk." Kids can be cruel. They didn't know me. Or what was really happening to me.

I definitely wasn't walking a straight line. Occasionally I was even banging into a locker. But I wasn't drunk. And I wished I could tell all the gossips how hard I tried to walk like a normal person; how much I wanted to write a letter without my hand trembling; how much I wanted to go a whole day without falling down. But if they asked me what was wrong, I'd have to tell them I didn't know. Not even the doctors knew.

And as time went by, it was to get drastically worse. But back then in school, I was making a painful discovery about serious illness that I hadn't expected: It makes you feel like an outsider in the human family. The sickness of your physical body can undermine your feelings of worth and usefulness. So you become sick in spirit too—at a time when you most need to feel close to God.

How to be spiritually well—how to regain my sense of wholeness and value—was a search that became as critical to me as finding ways to cope with my deteriorating health.

In 1965, I'd been a typical, active fifteen-year-old who loved gymnastics, played the flute in the high school orchestra, worked at an afterschool job, and headed the youth group at my church. But then weird things started happening. One day in gym class I couldn't get my left hand to grasp the flying rings. That night, I slipped on the stairs at home, and I slipped again the next day at school. "Just part of growing up," the doctor said. "Your symptoms will disappear in time." But they didn't.

So I lurched down hallways, every step taking me farther into the unknown. After a while came double vision, then a brace for a left arm that was turning more and more into itself. I underwent one test after another, but nothing led to a diagnosis. I started college but had to drop out; I wasn't well enough. My life became filled with more tests, more symptoms, more problems.

Finally, in 1970, my doctor had some concrete information for me. "We've identified your condition, Barbara," he said. "You have MS—multiple sclerosis. It usually doesn't strike people quite so young as yourself."

"What do we do now?" I asked.

My doctor shook his head. "I'll tell you the truth; there's almost nothing we can do. This disease is slowly going to short-circuit your central nervous system because it hardens the tissue around your brain and spine. The wrong messages go to various parts of your body, and they don't function as they should. The severity varies. We can only hope your case is a mild one."

Very soon, the course my MS was taking became clear. Twice, in 1971 and 1972, my heart and lungs failed, and I was rushed to the hospital, near death. Then there was a period of stability when I neither got better nor very much worse—a common occurrence in MS. I attended college as a handicapped student and later worked as a secretary. But the virulence of the disease was merely interrupted. I went from a cane to crutches. Inside my body, vital organs were beginning to fail. A partly paralyzed diaphragm made breathing difficult, and asthma and pneumonia became chronic problems. I needed a Foley catheter for bladder control and, when I lost bowel function, an ileostomy.

By 1978, I was in a wheelchair—my feet and hands curled and all but useless—and I required a constant supply of oxygen. That year, I went to the Mayo Clinic, hoping to discover new techniques to help my labored breathing. There weren't any. Clinic doctors didn't hold out false hope. "Pray, Barbara," they told me. "Nothing we can do will stop the deterioration."

Pray. A cliche? Not to me.

As a child of nine, I'd committed my life to Jesus. Then, as a teenager, I drifted away from the commitment until one of my doctors and his wife helped bring me close to God again. This happened when I was twenty, around the time my MS was diagnosed. Over the next few years my church pastor, Meredith Bailie, became a special friend, visiting me day after day in the hospital and when I was bedridden at home.

It was Pastor Bailie who helped me discover what I needed most: a goal. And the goal was to grow in faith. It became my "job," something I could do despite all the pain and loss of bodily capacity; and I worked at it. Sometimes I failed, gave up, lost God, asked "Why?" Yet always, no matter how low or sick or abandoned I felt, I'd eventually get a little spiritual nudge—a reminder of all the times I nearly died but didn't, of all the people in my church and community who were praying for me.

Now, after the grim visit to Mayo, I felt a new urgency about my connection to God. The less physical health I had, the more I yearned for spiritual health.

I cried out to God. "Please! Please! I can't even read your Word anymore. I need something to do."

Over and over I pleaded for something to counteract the fact that I could barely move. I craved activity. Action. I called out to God for it.

His answer came. Not in a flash, not overnight, but through prayer itself: *Praying is action. Pray for others.*

How simple. How possible! Until that thought came to me, I had seen prayer as passive. Now I saw that praying for others could be my gymnastics, my flute-playing, my special activity.

I had prayed for others before, but now it became a compelling need, a vocation. I spent hours in prayer, and more hours reading the Bible. When friends came over, I would ask them to read to me or pray with me. I talked to God, often out loud, as if he were standing right beside me.

My condition continued to worsen. A lung collapsed. Most of the time I could barely see; technically I was blind. In 1980, I had a tracheostomy, an incision made in my windpipe to allow a more direct connection to my oxygen supply My parents had made changes in our house to accommodate my needs—for my electric wheelchair, for a hospital bed, and for the tubing running through three rooms so I could hook up to my oxygen concentrator in different locations. Everyone knew I was dying. My doctors confirmed it. My mother and father and I began counseling with the Hospice Volunteers of Du Page County, a group that provides therapy for terminally ill patients and their families.

Then came June 7, 1981.

It was a Sunday, my sister Jan's twenty-ninth birthday. She was coming over to celebrate, and I looked forward to giving my mother at least some token help with making the cake. I remember thinking what a bright, clear day it was when my mother came into my room. "Ready to give the cake batter a few licks?" she asked. I nodded. With my mother helping, I began the struggle to hitch myself out of bed and into my wheelchair; my legs had begun drawing into a fetal position and it was impossible for me to put my feet flat on the floor. We transferred tubing on my tracheostomy to the oxygen supply mounted on my wheelchair and gathered my various receptacles around me, then I used my forearm to push down the starter lever on my wheelchair.

In the kitchen, I managed to stir the cake batter a couple of times despite the fact that my hands had turned inward to the point where my fingers almost touched my wrists. By now, even that small effort was enough to exhaust me, and I asked my mother to help me get back into bed. She did, and went back to finish the cake for Jan's birthday.

After a while, my Aunt Ruthie came to my room to read letters and cards from people who listened to a Chicago radio station, WMBI. A program called "Cup of Cold Water" had featured me as an invalid needing cheer. Most of the well-wishers mentioned that they were praying for me. My aunt left to help my mother, and shortly after noon, two friends, Joyce Jugan and Angela Crawford, popped in after the morning worship service at my church. Then, as the three of us visited, I heard a fourth voice. A firm, audible voice over my left shoulder.

"My child, get up and walk!" Startled, I looked at my friends. I could see that they had not heard the voice. But I was certain that I had heard it.

"Joyce! Angela!" I blurted, "God just spoke to me. He said to get up and walk. I heard him."

The two women stared at me.

"I know, I know, it's weird," I said. "But God really did speak to me. Please, run and get my family. I want them!"

They flew out to the hallway, called my sisters and parents, and rushed back into the room. I couldn't wait any longer. I took the oxygen tube from my throat, removed the brace from my arm, and actually jumped out of bed. And there I stood, on two legs that hadn't held the weight of my body in over five years.

This wasn't possible, of course—there were 1,001 medical reasons why this couldn't be happening. Yet there I stood, firmly, solidly, feeling tingly all over, as if I had just stepped from an invigorating shower. I could breathe freely. And I could see—I could see me. A whole, healthy me. My hands were normal, not curled to my wrists. The muscles in my arms and legs were filled out and whole. My feet were flat to the ground, like a dancer's. And oh, the steps I danced as I headed toward the doorway. I met my mother in the hallway. She stopped short and then she lifted the hem of my nightgown. Her eyes widened, her arms flung wide. "Barbara," she cried. "You have calves again!"

Dad was on the wheelchair ramp to the family room. Speechless, he wrapped me in his arms and waltzed me around and around. Then everyone—my parents, Aunt Ruthie, Jan, my teenage sister Amy—applauded wildly while I tried some ballet steps I hadn't done in sixteen years. Next I walked to the couch, sat down— and stood up again. Down. Up. Down. Up. Six times in a row.

Angela Crawford, an occupational therapist, hardly knew what she was saying: "B-but, Barb, you can't . . ." She took my pulse and exclaimed, "Barb, you've just wrecked everything I learned in school! You're absolutely normal; it's really a miracle!"

We praised God right there. Then quickly I went outside. Since my clothing was stored at my sister Jan's house, I went out into the front yard in my robe, reveling in the fresh green lawn under my bare feet, the warm sun on my cheek, the good, sweet air that filled my lungs. I could not believe the beauty of the spring flowers. I held them to my face and worshiped God.

Everyone promised to keep the incredible news a secret, and we made plans to slip into the evening service at church that night, after Jan's birthday dinner. It had been perhaps three years since I'd attended church. Pastor Bailie had visited me a week before and, I learned later, was convinced he would never again see me alive.

When I walked up the stairs to the Wheaton Wesleyan sanctuary that night, Pastor Bailie was asking the congregation if anyone had any announcements to make. Then he saw me walking down the aisle and fell against the pulpit, stunned. "This is nice, this is very nice," he kept repeating. When he composed himself, he invited me up to share the good news.

The next day I phoned my doctor's office. His nurse was puzzled. "You say this is Barbara Cummiskey? But—" When I walked into Dr. Thomas Marshall's office later that day, he stared as if he were seeing an apparition. He had never seen me up and walking and dressed.

For the next three hours, with other doctors invited in, Dr. Marshall put me through a series of tests and x-rayed my lungs. The film showed normal lungs; before, one lung had been collapsed and the other had been functioning at only fifty percent of its capacity.

Finally, Dr. Marshall shook his head in amazement. He found no signs of MS. He removed the tube in my neck, took out the catheter, and told me to forget my medications.

One of my surgeons, Dr. Harold Adolph, summed up my case in a written report: "At the present time, the patient has no findings of multiple sclerosis, walks normally, speaks normally, and is very happy, as is her family, over the obvious answer to prayer and the good hand of God in her life."

I don't know why God healed me. I don't believe I "earned" or "deserved" a healing any more than I "deserved" MS. I only know that on the morning of June 7, 1981, I felt good about myself—mentally, emotionally, and spiritually. Through my prayer life, I was a busy, active member of the human family—not running or jumping or even walking like most people, but not separated from them by bitterness, self-pity, or despair. My mind and spirit were healthy and whole.

And then God made my body whole too.

Prayer Convoy on I-70

Ron Lantz

September 2003

*T*raffic on I-70 wasn't too bad. I should have been enjoying myself that day last October, sitting up in the cab of my eighteen-wheeler, cruising through the Pennsylvania hills.

Thirty-six years as a trucker, and I still got a kick out of my rig. Bass Transportation bought this six-hundred-horsepower tractor in 2000. I was the only one who drove it, and although I'd logged almost four hundred thousand miles, the cab was still so clean you could eat off the floor. If traffic held steady, I would make my usual run right on schedule, hauling a tanker of building compound from Ohio to Delaware, then deadheading back to my home in Ludlow, Kentucky.

But I didn't make the run on time that day, for the same reason I wasn't enjoying the trip. The Beltway sniper. The words hammered in my head. Eight dead and two wounded already, and it didn't look like there'd be an end to it. At any truck stop in the D.C. area, all we talked about was the white van the police were looking for. Schools were closed, people too scared to leave their homes. It weighed on me that this guy was out there getting ready to kill again.

I knew what it was like to lose someone you love. Five years earlier my wife, Ruth, and I had lost our only son, Ron, to multiple sclerosis.

It was a pretty October day just like this one when he died. I knew when I got to the nursing home that something was up because there was a lot of hollering down the hall. "What's going on?" I asked.

"It's your son, Mr. Lantz," a nurse said.

I hurried to Ron's room. There was our boy sitting on the edge of his bed, hands raised over his head, praising the Lord. For more than a year he hadn't been able to sit up on his own.

"I'm leaving here," Ron said. "Someone's coming through that door tonight to take me home." Then he looked at me real hard. "Dad, I don't want to be up in heaven waiting for you and you don't make it."

It wasn't the first time he'd brought up the subject. Ron was a real committed Christian. My parents raised me in the faith, but somehow I'd drifted away. "I want you to go over to my church right now," Ron went on. "Find my pastor and give your life to the Lord."

Well, that's exactly what I did. Afterward I went back to the nursing home and told Ron. I'm glad I had the chance, because Somebody did come for my boy that night to take him home.

My life turned around. I got active in church. I headed the men's fellowship, led retreats, was on the Sunday school board,

I'd never start a run without kneeling by my bed at the rear of the cab and asking God to watch over Ruth.

After the sniper shot his first victims, I'd been praying about that too—that someone would stop this killing spree. It had gone on for twelve days already. Around seven P.M., when I was about an hour and a half out of Wilmington, Delaware, the usual report came on the radio. Nothing new on the sniper. All they knew was that a white van might be involved.

I got to thinking about what I'd learned at church, how a bunch of people praying together can be more powerful than a person praying alone. *What if I get on my CB, see if a few drivers want to pull off the road with me and pray about this?*

I pressed the button on my microphone and said that if anyone wanted to pray about the sniper, he could meet me in half an hour at the eastbound 66-mile-marker rest area. A trucker answered right away. Then another and another. They'd be there. I hadn't gone five miles before a line of trucks formed, some coming up from behind, others up ahead slowing down to join us. The line stretched for miles.

It was getting dark when we pulled into the rest area. There must have been fifty rigs there. We all got out of our cabs and stood in a circle, holding hands, sixty or seventy of us, including some wives and children.

"Let's pray," I said. "Anyone who feels like it can start." Well, the first one to speak up was a kid about ten years old, standing just to my left. The boy bowed his head: "Our Father, who art in heaven. . . ."

We went around the circle, some folks using their own

words, others using phrases from the Lord's Prayer. It seemed to me there was a special meaning where it says " . . . deliver us from evil. . . ."

The last person finished. We had prayed for fifty-nine minutes. All those truckers adding an hour to their busy schedules!

Ten days later, on October 23, I was making my Ohio-to-Delaware run again. There had been another killing and the sniper was no nearer to being caught.

Right from the start there was something different about my trip. In the first place, it was a Wednesday. I normally made my runs Tuesdays and Thursdays. But there had been a delay at the loading dock so I told my pastor I'd have to miss our Wednesday night prayer meeting. "We'll be praying for you," he said.

The second thing that happened was being stopped by the cops. Once was rare for me. This trip I was pulled over three times. Not for very long—they were just checking papers—but it made me late getting into Wilmington.

Then, instead of catching a few hours of sleep, I headed back west as soon as my cargo was offloaded around eleven P.M. That wasn't like me at all. I knew too many sad stories about drivers didn't get enough sleep. But it was like I had an appointment I was anxious about, like I couldn't sleep even if I tried.

At midnight the "Truckin' Bozo" show came on the air, a music and call-in program a lot of truckers listen to. There was news in the sniper case. There were two snipers, not one, and police now believed the guys were driving a blue 1990 Chevrolet Caprice with New Jersey plates, license number NDA–21Z. Not the white van we had all been looking for.

I wrote down the tag number. Just before one A.M., I reached the rest stop at the 39-mile-marker near Myersville, Maryland, only a few miles from where so many of us had made a circle and prayed. Westbound on I-70, this was the only rest area between Baltimore and Breezewood with a men's room. I wasn't going to pass that by.

And here was the last weird thing about that trip: the truck aisles were full. I'd never seen so many rigs at that stop, drivers asleep. The only thing I could do was swing around to the car section. I wouldn't be long. Climbing down from my cab, I noticed a car in the No Parking zone. The light over the men's room door was shining right on it.

A blue Chevrolet Caprice.

There must be hundreds of blue Caprices out there. I looked closer: two men, one slumped over the wheel, asleep. Beyond the men's room was a row of bushes. I crept behind them and squinted to make out the license number. Jersey plates. N . . . DA2 . . . 1 . . . Z.

As quietly as I could, I climbed back in my rig. I decided it was better not to use the CB in case those guys have one. I punched 911 on my cell phone. "I'm at the Myersville rest stop. There's a blue Chevrolet Caprice here, Jersey license NDA–21Z."

The operator asked me to hold. In a minute she came back with instructions. "Wait there. Don't let them see you. Block the exit with your truck if you can."

If an eighteen-wheeler can tiptoe, that's what mine did. I blocked as much of the exit ramp as I could, but there was still room for a car to get by. Five minutes passed. Only one other driver was ready to roll. As soon as I told him what was happening, he pulled his rig alongside mine, sealing off the exit. I sat in my cab, looking out the side mirrors at that blue Caprice, expecting a shootout, thinking I ought to be scared and wondering why I wasn't.

Five more minutes passed. I was afraid another truck or a car would drive up and honk for us to move, waking the suspects, but no one stirred. The cops slid up so quietly that I didn't know they were there. Suddenly it was like the Fourth of July, with flash grenades lighting up the night to stun the two men.

FBI agents, state troopers, and officers from the sheriff's department swarmed the rest stop. Searchlights. Breaking glass. Shouts. The thump of helicopters, SWAT teams in Night Vision goggles, running low, crouching, guns drawn.

The next thing I knew, the two men were being led away. The police took down the names and addresses of everyone who had been at the rest area. It was two and a half hours before we were free to go. Since I'd been blocking the exit, I was the first one out.

Five miles down the road, I started shaking so badly I could hardly hold the wheel. Then I got to thinking about all the unusual things that had to happen for me to be at that place at that time, and about my friends at church praying for me that same evening. And I couldn't help thinking about my son, Ron, who'd led me to that church.

I looked in my rearview mirror at the line of trucks behind me and remembered leading another line of semis ten days earlier. I remembered the circle of truckers and their families, holding hands, voices joined together to pray, " . . . deliver us from evil."

On the Wings of Faith

My Friend God

ELAINE ST. JOHNS

January 1951

My daughter, Kristen, has just turned six years old. She is a thoroughly joyous being who inhabits a small, tanned body and inspects the world with curiosity through unperturbed blue eyes.

During her day of play, it is very hard to tell when she is my daughter and when she is pretending to be someone else—Brave Heart, Gretel, or Hoppy.

Every so often, because of her high regard for the truth and to keep the record straight between us, she reassures me.

"It's only a pretend, Mommy," she confides. "I'm really your little girl, Kristen."

But she has one special friend with whom no liberties are taken. That is "my Friend God."

She introduced him into our daily living when she was five. Sitting on the living room floor in a pool of sunbeams, Kristie seemed absorbed in coloring. It should have been a quiet Sunday afternoon. But the radio volume had been nudged higher and higher so the "head of the house" could hear the ball game above the noises that Kristie's brother, Koko, and I were making.

Suddenly, over the din, Kristie's voice rose.

"My Friend God wants me to have peace," she pleaded.

In the abashed silence that followed, Kristie didn't even look up. She continued her art work.

Since then, I, who introduced them, have been humble before their ripening friendship. Humble, too, before the unfailing simplicity with which she approaches him.

Where did she get her facts about God? She got them from the usual sources: Bible stories we read at home, Psalms we say together, the little Sunday school where she and her playmates learn hymns. But the interpretation is strictly her own.

She has found that her Heavenly Father is always around, something she cannot truthfully say of her earthly parents. She is sure he created all things good and beautiful, hence he is a powerful ally, fully capable of assisting her with any problem. He has never let her down.

Take the matter of her red wagon. Did we, or did we not, lose it? One day it is in its usual place; the next day it is gone

We search diligently in all the possible places on our four acres. We ask Koko. We ask Grandma. We have done our best but we do not find it.

"Well," advises Kristie matter-of-factly: "we'd better ask God."

And because her blue eyes are fastened trustfully on mine, I sit down on the stone wall beside her and we ask. But I'm afraid it won't work.

Suddenly we are drawn to look in the coal shed, an unlikely place for the red wagon at any time—but especially during summer months.

We go to look. It is there. We hug each other, rejoicing.

Scrambling into the wagon and pushing off with one foot, Kristie says, "Thanks, God."

Or take the afternoon our terrace is inexplicably littered with broken flower pots where our hanging garden has come tumbling down.

"Kristen," says Grandma very kindly, "Did you accidentally knock down these pots while playing?"

"No, Grandma." Her tight little braids shake emphatically.

"Kristie, are you sure?"

"I didn't break them, Grandma." She wants very much to be believed. "Ask God," she tells her grandmother.

Two hours later we catch the neighbor's cat whisking off the rest of the pots with a playful paw.

Her Friend seems to have taught her a simple, infallible rule for brotherly love. Kristie simply sizes people up as either "close to God," like George Washington who never told a lie, or people who "don't know about God yet," like a man she once saw on the street who was quite drunk.

She has a good-natured tolerance for those of us who "get away" from God temporarily by losing such human things as tempers or self-control. For there are times when she herself is not on the very best of terms with her Friend.

"Some days," she explains thoughtfully, "I just want to do what I want to do. I don't want to listen to him."

These are very unpleasant days, crammed with tears and punishments; and I am always grateful when she has had enough and creeps quietly into her room to "get close" to him again. I do not know if she talks to him, or listens to him, or prays. These matters are between her and her Friend.

On the adult plane where we scientific parents dwell, all this could be charming and well-laced with coincidence—except for one fact. Like the mountain climber who does not know the quality of the rope until he has fallen, so it is with my daughter's faith in her Friend. For she fell off the side of a mountain, and her rope held. Actually, it was a small mountain.

Kristie had her bad spill while carrying a small glass bottle. A razor-sharp fragment from the broken glass cut deeply into the palm of her hand. When I reached her side, the blood was gushing upward in a terrifying, irregular fountain. I used my fingers as a tourniquet, and soon she lay quietly in my lap while we contacted the Emergency Hospital.

"I want to make a prayer," she told Grandma in a small voice, "but I haven't any words. You make the words, Grandma." But because Grandma's words were slow in coming, traveling as they must around a big, grown-up lump of emotion, Kristie patiently made her own prayer.

"God," she said, "You love me. Even if all the blood runs out, you are my life, and I love you."

In that confidence she rested.

At the hospital, the cool young doctor refused to perform the necessary surgery while I was in the room. My daughter lay there, very small in her bloody jeans, with her four freckles standing out on her little pug nose. I could not bear leaving her to face the ordeal alone.

"You just wait in the hall like the doctor says, Mommy," she advised.

Forty minutes later I re-entered the room. "Everything in her hand was laid wide open," the doctor said gravely. "But your daughter has full use of all her fingers. No permanent damage. It was a miracle."

"It wasn't a miracle," said my little daughter firmly.

"It was my Friend God."

The Blessed Assurance

NORMAN VINCENT PEALE

April 1963

All members of the human race have two things in common: each of us was born and each of us must die. Most of us are not too concerned with the circumstances of our birth. We don't remember it, it lies far behind us. But the thought of dying is another matter. The knowledge that our days on this earth will come to an end is an inescapable part of our existence—somber, mysterious, and sometimes frightening.

Quite often people come to me and confess that they are haunted by a fear of death that they try to conceal from other people, and even from themselves. These people are not necessarily old or ill. Often they are in the prime of life, with many useful years ahead of them. But sometimes it seems that the more they love life, the more they dread death.

What I usually do with such people is admit that I, too, have moments when I flinch from the thought of dying. I suggest that this is perfectly natural, that in my opinion the good Lord planted a certain amount of this fear in all of us so that we would not be tempted to relinquish the trials and responsibilities of this life too easily. But, I add, I'm sure the Lord didn't intend us to be panicky about it. Finally, I try to reassure these troubled souls by outlining the thoughts that have helped me rise above the fear of death, or at least keep it under control.

Take, for example, the inevitability of dying. This seems to appall some people, but it always has struck me as a merciful thing. Suppose there were loopholes in this universal law; suppose that somehow there was a one percent chance of avoiding death. Consider how frantically we'd search for that loophole and how wretched we'd be not to find it.

Now consider how wretched we'd be if we did find it! No one would be happy trying to live forever. It's a little like being at a wonderful play. During the performance, one hopes that it will go on and on, but one wouldn't really like to stay in the theater all night.

Another thing I tell the worried ones is this: you may be frightened in advance, but it is almost certain that when the time comes, you will not fear death at all. I have talked to doctors and nurses who have seen hundreds of people die, and they all tell me that at the end, unless they are tormented by a guilty conscience, people go peacefully and thankfully. The truth is, death has been miscast as a grim reaper. To almost everyone, when it finally comes, it comes as a friend.

"That may be true," say some of the fearful ones. "The moment of death may be less terrifying than we thought. But then what? Is there a life after death? Is there any proof?"

To these I reply, "It depends on what you mean by proof. To me the evidence is overwhelming, whether you consult your reason or your instincts. Look at the vast universe that surrounds us, the laws that govern the spinning solar systems and the whirling electrons, the balance and economy of a stupendous reality that uses everything and wastes nothing. Does it seem reasonable that the Intelligence behind such a reality would create a being as complex and sensitive as man just to snuff him out forever like the flame of a candle? Of course it doesn't!"

What is death, then? Obviously it is a change into some new form of existence. We are not permitted to know exactly what this new existence is like, but I believe that sometimes we are given glimpses. Time and again we have been told of people on the brink of death who seem to become aware of a great radiance, or hear beautiful music, or see the faces of departed loved ones who are waiting for them. Are these just hallucinations? I don't think so. Several of these experiences have happened within my own family.

My father, who died at eighty-five after a distinguished career as both physician and minister, struggled against a very real fear of death. But not long after he died, my stepmother dreamed that he came to her and told her that his fears had been groundless.

"Don't ever worry about dying," he said to her. "There's nothing to it!" The dream was so vivid that she woke up, astounded. And I believe that my father did come to reassure her, because that is precisely the phrase I have heard him use a thousand times to dismiss something as unimportant or trivial.

In 1939 when news reached me that my mother had died unexpectedly in another town, I was alone in my office, numb with grief and loss. There was a Bible on my desk, and I put my hand on it, staring blindly out of the window. As I did so, I unmistakably felt a pair of hands touch my head, gently, lovingly. The pressure lasted only an instant, then it was gone. An illusion? A hallucination caused by grief? I don't think so. I think my mother was permitted to reach across the gulf of death to touch and reassure me.

Just last year, when I was preaching at a Methodist gathering in Georgia, I had the most startling experience of all. At the end of the final session, the presiding bishop asked all the ministers in the audience to come forward, form a choir, and sing an old, familiar hymn.

I was sitting on the speakers' platform, watching them come down the aisles. And suddenly, among them, I saw my father. I saw him as plainly as I ever saw him when he was alive. He seemed about forty, vital and handsome. He was singing with the others. When he smiled at me, and put up his hand in the old familiar gesture, for several unforgettable seconds it was as if my father and I were alone in that big auditorium. Then he was gone, but in my heart the certainty of his presence was indisputable. He was there, and I know that some day, somewhere, I'll meet him again.

We don't try to prove immortality so that we can believe in it; we try to prove it because we cannot help believing in it. Instinct whispers to us that death is not the end. Reason supports it. Psychic phenomena uphold it. Even science, in its own way, now insists that the universe is more spiritual than material. Einstein's great equation indicates that matter and energy are interchangeable. Where does that leave us, if not in an immaterial universe? The great psychologist William James said, "Apparently there is one great universal mind, and since man enters into this universal mind, he is a fragment of it."

This intangible in all of us, this fragment of the universal mind, is what religion calls the soul. And it is indestructible because—as James said—it is at one with God. The Founder of Christianity said specifically that there is a life beyond the grave. Not only that, Jesus proved it by rising from the dead himself. If you believe that it happened, death should hold little terror for you. If you don't believe it, you are not a completely fulfilled Christian.

The Easter message is one of such hope and joy that even unbelievers are thrilled by it. Last year a reporter I know covered the sunrise service that is held each Easter on the rim of the Grand Canyon. It was cold—below freezing, actually—and he had not worn an overcoat. Not a particularly religious man, he stood there shivering dolefully and wishing himself back in bed.

"But then," he told me, "when the sun cleared the canyon rim, and light poured into that stupendous chasm, I forgot all about being cold. One moment everything was gray and form-less. Then came torrents of light plunging down the canyon walls, making them blaze with color, dissolving the blackness into pur-ple shadows that eddied like smoke. Standing there, I had a most indescribable feeling, a conviction that the darkness that had filled the great gorge was an illusion—that only the light was real, and that we silent watchers on the canyon rim were somehow a part of the light."

These were strange words, coming from a hard-boiled reporter, but close to a profound truth. Darkness is powerless before the onslaught of light. And so it is with death. We have allowed ourselves to think of it as a dark door, when actually it is a rainbow bridge spanning the gulf between two worlds.

That is the Easter message. Yet there are people, even good Christians, who accept it with their minds but really never feel it in their hearts. I know this from personal experience: the message never got through fully to me until I went to the Holy Land and saw with my own eyes the hills and fields and roads where Jesus actually walked.

One day we visited the beautiful little village of Bethany. This was the home of Mary and Martha and Lazarus. And there is still a tomb there that is said to be the tomb of Lazarus. We went into that tomb, down twenty-two steps, and saw the place where the body of Lazarus is presumed to have lain until the voice of Jesus wakened him from the dead. I was so deeply moved that when we came up out of the tomb, I turned to my wife and said, "We are standing where the greatest statement ever uttered was made. 'I am the resurrection, and the life: he that believeth in me, though he were dead, yet shall he live.'"

At that moment, for the first time in my life, Easter really happened to me, and I shall never be the same again. For the rest of my days I shall preach, out of a conviction so deep that it can never be shaken, that if people will accept Jesus Christ, they will have eternal life.

Recently, I was at Mount Holyoke College in New England, visiting my daughter Elizabeth. Walking around the campus, we came upon a sundial. On it was an inscription: *To larger sight, the rim of shadow is the line of light.*

There you have it in just twelve words. Believe me, death is only a momentary rim of shadow. Beyond it, waiting for all of us who deserve it, is the radiance of eternal life.

His Mysterious Ways

TUESDAY NIGHT was chicken night at the restaurant where I worked as a waitress, but on this Tuesday few customers ordered it. "Take some home," said the manager. The chicken was greasy, so I wrapped it in plastic, a box, and a bag.

The last customers lingered, and we closed late. Having missed the last bus, I began walking home through deserted Milwaukee streets. Unable to afford a cab, I prayed and sang a hymn. God would see me home safely.

But he didn't. A man with a knife leaped out of the shadows, pushed me down a dark side street, and spoke in ugly language of what he'd do when we reached his place on Brady Street. Why had God forsaken me?

Despite my anger, I kept praying. And then, out of nowhere I heard four words. They were very clear, very firm. "Debbie, eat your chicken." What? Was I losing my mind? "Debbie, eat your chicken."

As I was being dragged along, I pulled out a chicken breast, struggling with all the wrappings. Crying too hard to eat, I just carried it in my hand. Soon we reached Brady Street.

Two large dogs rummaged in spilled trash cans. Suddenly the dogs perked their heads and sniffed the air. Growling and baring teeth, they charged at us. My attacker fled.

The dogs did not lunge at me. They fixed their eyes on the chicken in my hand. I tore off meat and threw it down, where they fought hungrily for it. Dropping pieces every few yards, I got the stray dogs to follow me home. By the time I was safely inside, I'd begun to understand. *Debbie, eat your chicken*—the chicken that had been wrapped too thickly to be smelled by even a dog. But in my hand . . .

—DEBORAH ROSE, *September 1985*

The Woman Who
Wasn't Afraid

LOUISE DEGRAFINRIED

October 1984

*E*very time I heard a noise outside—a snap of twigs, a rus-
tle of leaves—I found myself at the kitchen window, peering out into the dark, wet February night. Maybe it was one of
them, making the noise. Maybe the four of them were hiding out
in the marshy bottomland behind our house.

"Do you really think they're nearby?" I said once more to
my husband, Nathon.

"Well, that's what the television says," he replied. Indeed, it
had. Three days earlier, we'd heard the first report. Five men had
escaped from the Fort Pillow State Prison, just forty miles north
of us. The men were armed, desperate, and very dangerous. They
were murderers and rapists. They didn't have much to lose,
either; some were already serving life sentences. Then one was
caught. And the police had figured the rest of them were hiding

out somewhere in the rural bottomland between Mason and Braden in southwest Tennessee.

That's right by us. Mason is five miles away; Braden, a little nearer. But the bottoms are all around us. Out nearest neighbor lives a good piece away—certainly out of hollering distance.

The leaves rustled again. No, it was just the cold winter wind, maybe a possum or two. "Nathon," I said, "what would we do if those men came here?"

"Honey," Nathon replied, "we'd do what they said."

I didn't like the idea of people hanging around outside my house at all. "Nathon, pull down that shade in the bathroom," I said. We hadn't done that for as long as I could remember. We didn't have to, living so far out like we did. But tonight was different.

It wasn't that I didn't feel safe. I always feel safe in our house, because our house is God's house too. Nathon and I raised four children in it with no troubles. And I just knew that was because our house is a house of prayer.

I learned about God and about praying when I was growing up with my Grandpa Dempsey. We lived with him after my father died when I was just five years old. More than any other person I've ever known, Grandpa Dempsey depended on God. Every night at nine o'clock, he would get the whole family together in a circle for prayer. "If you trust in God, then he will take care of you," I remember him saying to us. "Look at me. I raised eighteen children and I never paid no fine for any of them." Oh, Grandpa believed all right. He taught me to believe too.

I was glad to see the sun the next morning. It had been a cold night. When I looked out the kitchen window, there was still frost on the ground.

"Nathon, you put Cat outside while I'm cooking. How many eggs do you want?" And I just kept on talking. I'm always the one talking in this family. Every once in a while, Nathon said, "Uh-huh."

We had just finished eating when the phone rang. It was my good friend Renzie Fields. She wanted to know if we'd heard about the escaped cons on TV.

"Renzie, we did," I said. And we talked about it for a few minutes. Once, I put my hand over the receiver. "Nathon, I hear Cat crying. Better let him back in."

I'd gone back to talking with Renzie when I heard Nathon holler, "Honey, open the door. Open the door!"

That startled me. Nathon didn't ever raise his voice unless there was an awfully good reason.

I just couldn't imagine what would make Nathon holler like that, unless . . .

"Honey, open the door!" he hollered.

"Renzie," I said softly, "call the police." And quickly I hung up. Even as I put the receiver down, I wondered if Renzie would know what in the world I meant.

I hurried across the kitchen and flung the door open fast as I could. There in front of me stood a tall black man. His clothes were covered with mud. He had a dirty sock tied around his neck.

And he had a huge shotgun jabbed into my Nathon's side.

"Don't make me shoot you, old man," he growled. He motioned Nathon into the house, and then quickly followed him through the door. Nathon stumbled over the garbage can, but I grabbed his arm, and then we both stood back in a corner, watching the man closely. His eyes darted about, looking all over our small house. "Are you looking for company today?" he demanded.

"No," I said, "nobody's coming here."

"Good. Where's the telephone?" I pointed to it. He reached over, snatched the receiver off the hook and dropped it on the chair. Then he turned and began looking about the house again like he was trying to find a place to hide.

Where are the others? I wondered. *Are they lurking out of sight waiting?*

"I was outside your house all night. I could hear you folks talking about me," the man said. "Old man, does that truck of yours run? I'm gonna want you to give me a ride." Then he turned around toward us. "Well?"

"All right, then, I'll give you a ride," Nathon said. "But sometimes the old truck doesn't crank. I'll have to go outside and see if it will start."

The man was quiet for a moment. There was no change in his expression, his steely-eyed gaze. "Okay, go ahead. But don't try anything funny. Don't make me shoot you, old man. Or her!" And he waved his gun at me. Nathon went outside slowly.

Armed, desperate, very dangerous, the TV report had said. *Murderers and rapists, lifers with nothing to lose.* And now I was looking down the barrel of a shotgun held by one of these men. *Murderers* . . . his finger was still on the trigger.

"Young man," I said, and I took a few steps toward him. "I am . . ."

"Get back," he barked, pointing the shotgun boldly in front of him. "I already told you, don't make me do nothing."

You'd think by this time I would have been scared out of my wits, but I wasn't. In fact, I was a little mad. That young man had barged into our house, and he had no right to do it. I wasn't going to let that man harm us either. Not in this house, because this was God's house. And God wasn't going to let anything happen to us in it.

"Young man," I said again, this time not moving. "I'm a Christian lady. We don't have any violence in this house. This is God's house. Put that gun down."

There was silence. He looked at me for a long time. No words. He held the gun perfectly still, pointed right at me.

"I said, 'Put that gun down!'" Then slowly he turned, bent over, and leaned the gun up against the couch. And he slumped on the couch himself.

"Lady, I am so hungry," he said. "I haven't eaten in three days."

"Then I will fix you breakfast," I said. The fixings were still on the counter from when Nathon and I had eaten. I started cracking eggs in a bowl.

"What's your name, young man?"

"Riley," he said. I found out he was twenty-six years old. He came from Texas. And he was serving twenty-five years for murder. "But I didn't do it," he said.

I put down a plate of eggs, bacon, and toast on the table in front of him, along with a half-gallon jug of milk. "All right," I said, "say something."

Riley just looked at me funny. I guessed they didn't say grace in prison. But in Nathon's and my house, we said it. And we always said it with a Bible verse. But, I thought, maybe Riley doesn't know a Bible verse. Right then I thought of one for him, the shortest verse in the Bible.

"While you're here with us," I said, "say, 'Jesus wept.'"

Riley lowered his head. "Jesus wept," he mumbled.

I patted his leg, and I kept my hand there as I bowed my head and finished blessing the food for him. "Young man," I said when I was finished, "enjoy your breakfast. And when you're done, I'll fix up a solution to help your throat."

Riley looked at me, surprised. I knew he was wondering how I knew there was something wrong with his throat. But the moment he came in, I'd seen that sock tied around his neck. That's an old remedy my grandma taught me to take away a sore throat on a cold night.

"You sound like my grandmother," Riley said, taking a long swallow of milk.

"Where's your grandmother?" I said.

"She's dead," he replied.

"She loved you though, didn't she?" Riley looked at me and I thought I saw him nod. "Well, I love you, and I'm not dead. Jesus loves you too. He died for us all. That's the way I know he loves you."

Riley didn't say anything to that, but I just kept on giving him the Bible. And he just kept on eating. He hardly even noticed Nathon come back in, then go out and head down the front driveway.

"Young man, you'd like to give yourself up, wouldn't you?" I asked during one moment of silence.

He really looked scared when I said that. "Oh, lady," he said, "they'd kill me. They'd kill me in a minute."

"No," I said firmly, "they won't kill you. Not here. There won't be any violence in this house, by anyone."

Riley paused a minute. He must have been thinking about what I'd said. Then slowly, he nodded his head. "Okay. But tell just one to come. Just one."

"All right," I said. I stood up to reach the phone. Just then I saw them through the front window. There were four police cars in out driveway. Nathon was talking to a policeman. Riley saw me staring, and he jumped out of his chair and looked out the window too.

"Oh, lady, they're gonna kill me. There's going to be shooting." His voice quivered a little bit now. He looked back at his shotgun by the couch.

"Young man, you come and sit back down," I said. "They aren't going to kill you. Not if I do the talking."

The front door swung open and Nathon came in. "Honey, the police said for me and you to come out."

"All right," I said to Nathon. "I'll go out. But I want you to stay here and sit next to the young man." I turned to Riley. "Don't you worry. Nobody's going to hurt you."

I closed my eyes a second and prayed hard to the Lord. Then I stepped out the front door. The police came running from all directions. "Hold it right there!" I shouted to them. "Yes, that young man is in my house. But he's not violent now. He's not even sitting near that gun."

"Tell him to come out of the house with his hands behind his head," one of the police told me.

"All right," I said, "but you folks just stand back." I called into the house. "Nathon, tell him to come out with his hands behind his head. And Nathon, you come out right beside him."

So Nathon and Riley came down the steps together, and when they reached the bottom, the police put the handcuffs on Riley. Then they went back into the house to get Riley's shotgun. It was still leaning up against the couch, right where he had put it.

The police took Riley back to prison. I don't know what's happened to him since, but I'm praying for him. And I found out Renzie Fields did understand what I was saying on the telephone. She told me she found the sheriff that morning having coffee at the local truck stop.

Things are pretty much back to normal now, except that I've gotten a little more attention than an old countrywoman should expect. But I just tell everyone the same thing about not being scared of Riley. It's the truth of what happened. It was the Lord's doing that day. He takes care of you just like he says. I know, because he's always been right there with me. And he still is.

39,000 Feet over Florida

CAPTAIN O. A. FISH

September 1986

ormally on the Eastern Airlines Boston-Miami flight that I captain, we follow the eastern coastline to Wilmington, North Carolina, then go down Atlantic Route 1, a shortcut over water to Miami. But on the morning of January 28, 1986, that route would have taken us into the flight pattern of the space shuttle *Challenger*. So when I took my place at the controls of our Boeing 757, I was not surprised that we had been re-routed to stay over land and fly down the coastline airway.

We had 135 passengers on board and were ready to go, but the delay in launching the *Challenger* was delaying us too. From time to time I informed the passengers of the reasons for the holdup. I expected some to grumble, irritated at the time loss; however, for once everyone seemed to understand. They were interested in this particular launching, especially because it was to carry the first civilian into space, schoolteacher Christa McAuliffe.

At last we received permission to take off, and for a while

the flight went according to plan. South of Wilmington, however, there was a change. Air Traffic Control had just turned us off course on a radar vector, when I heard one of the other pilots on the frequency ask, "Did the spacecraft take off yet?"

There was a pause. Then came the controller's answer.

"Yes . . . but . . . it blew up one minute into flight."

There was stunned silence on the frequency.

Then someone broke in, "Did you just say what I thought you said?"

". . . Yes, I'm afraid so."

My copilot, Barney Ross, and I sat there staring silently into the open space ahead of us. Then the words began to tumble out.

"No!"

"It can't be . . . not all those people . . ."

"I don't believe it!"

Halting, inadequate expressions of disbelief and denial. Then slowly we each drifted back into our own private silence.

My thoughts turned to our passengers. Boston was a regional airport for the Northeast. There might be friends or relatives of Christa McAuliffe on the plane. I couldn't make an announcement like that cold over the PA system. It wasn't like pointing out a landmark below.

But what was I supposed to do? I had a small community of people back there who deserved to know. Yet how could I know what kind of effect the news would have on them? If I had been back home, I would have known what to do. I would have prayed with my friends and members from my church. But that was different. There in my own community, close to the people I knew, we could have reached out to God for comfort and assurance. But this was a Boeing 757 filled with people I'd never seen before.

Should I tell them or wait until we landed? I talked it over with Barney and the senior flight attendant. They thought I should wait. But the final decision was up to me. I was still trying to decide what to do when I was handed a note from a passenger. He was writing a letter to send to the Eastern management complimenting our crew on the flight. He said we had done a superb job, and that he liked the way I had kept them informed about what was going on with the space shuttle and the reasons for the delay.

Barney tapped me on the shoulder. I looked up from the note, my eyes following his gaze. There was a large cloud, a white vapor giant standing starkly against the naked blue Florida sky. It was different from normal clouds. I knew it was the one formed by the spacecraft explosion. And in that moment I also knew that I had to tell the passengers. In the past I had asked God to help me minister to people during times of need on my flights, and this was one of those times. I'd have to trust him to help me.

"Is there a minister on board?" I asked the senior attendant. She checked the passenger list. Yes, the Reverend J. B. Gauthier, a Jesuit priest, was seated near the rear.

"Go back and call him aside." I told her. "Tell him the news and ask if he would be willing to provide spiritual assistance should we need it."

The senior attendant came back soon and said the priest had agreed that I should make the announcement. "And," she said, "he'll be willing to help in any way he can."

I glanced once more out the window as the ominous cloud

drew closer, then I turned back to the senior attendant. "Would you ask him to lead us in a prayer after I make the announcement?" I asked. She nodded.

I picked up the microphone and switched it on. "Ladies and gentlemen, I have some very distressing news," I began. "I'm sorry to have to tell you . . . that the spaceship *Challenger* . . . has been destroyed." I struggled to force the words out. "It exploded just after takeoff."

We were over Daytona Beach, and as I banked the plane, the huge cloud floated up into the passengers' view. I switched off my mike as Father Gauthier began reading the 23rd Psalm over the flight attendant's PA system:

"The Lord is my shepherd; I shall not want. Fresh and green are the pastures where he gives me repose," he read. "Near restful waters he leads me. . . ." By now we were passing over Cape Canaveral, and we could see a long, dark snake-like stain stretching out over the ocean, probably the residue of unburned fuel.

". . . to revive my drooping spirit. He guides me along the right paths; he is true to his name. If I should walk in the valley of darkness . . ." The shadow of the huge cloud had fallen across the plane by now, blocking the sun.

". . . no evil would I fear. You are there with your crook and your staff; with these you give me comfort. You have prepared a banquet for me in the sight of my foes. My head you have anointed with oil; my cup is overflowing. . . ." As the cloud passed from sight, sunlight once again streamed through the windows. ". . . Surely goodness and kindness shall follow me all the days of my life. In the Lord's house shall I dwell for ever and ever."

Father Gauthier prayed for the astronauts and for their families. Even though I couldn't see them from the cockpit, I knew that every head on our plane was bowed and every heart touched.

After we'd landed in Miami, I left the cockpit as soon as possible to meet the man whose prayer had helped us all. As I looked at Father Gauthier standing beside me, I thought how different he was from my small-town Assembly of God preacher at home—and yet how alike in his concern for others.

Together we watched the passengers disembark. A mother slipped her arm around her young colt of a son as he stepped into the aisle in front of her, and for an instant, so quick I almost missed it, he laid his head against her shoulder. An older couple held hands as they inched down the aisle. A businessman put his attaché case on the seat and turned to help a college kid gather his gear. For once, no one seemed to be in a hurry to make a connection or catch the first cab. The passengers walked slowly out the door, some still wiping their eyes, others reaching out to lift a heavy bag or help with a sleepy child.

Young, old, men, women—I watched as this small sampling of mankind left the plane. Several passengers shook my hand; others expressed their appreciation to Father Gauthier. It was almost as if we were leaving a church after a touching service.

I knew none of us would ever forget where we were that day in January when *Challenger* exploded. In yet another time of national crisis, we'd found how much we needed one another, how much we needed and depended upon God. And I knew that we'd never feel closer to God than when we were part of that prayer meeting thirty-nine thousand feet high in the Florida sky.

Embracing the Joyful Life

Just a Bend in the Road

HELEN STEINER RICE

October 1976

Twice in my lifetime I thought my world had come to an end. I thought that all meaning and purpose were gone and that there was no reason to go on living. Yet, in both cases, what I did not know was that God had something excitingly new in store for me—that he would actually use those devastating personal losses to lift my soul into a new spiritual consciousness and lead my life into new areas of service I never would have dreamed possible.

Of course, I couldn't see any good in either of those heart-breaking experiences at the time. We never can. But now, with the luxury of a full life's experiences behind me, I am no longer looking at the back side of the tapestry; and I see much more clearly how all sorts of adversity—defeat, loneliness, disappointment, rejection, illness—can be used as a spring-board to spiritual triumph.

The bitterest pills I've had to swallow both dealt with the death of loved ones. The first came when I was sixteen and a senior in high school. It was doubly traumatic, because it came so suddenly and because it was set against the backdrop of an unbelievably secure and happy childhood.

I grew up in Lorain, Ohio, a bustling steel town on the shores of Lake Erie. My dad was a railroad engineer for the Baltimore & Ohio, which was a good job, but not so good that it elevated us above our neighbors. Dad was a warm, gentle man with an amazingly wide sphere of friends.

Mother was a dedicated homemaker and a gifted seamstress. Mother, my sister, and I were usually candidates for the fashion magazines when we strolled Reid Avenue on our way to 20th Street Methodist Church each Sunday.

Then suddenly, in the fall of 1918, Dad became ill. A flu epidemic was sweeping the country, taking many lives. In a matter of days, he was gone, another flu victim.

The great emptiness I felt the night of his death still causes something to stir inside me. I was so young, so vulnerable, so unaccepting. Standing on the back porch of our Reid Avenue house that cold, windy October night, I can remember sobbing over and over, "Why, why, God?"

Instead of going off to Ohio Wesleyan to study law as I'd planned, I went to work. Though we were not destitute, I wanted to stay close to home to help. My job was with the Ohio Public Service Company, doing an odd assortment of assignments at first, until I was asked to become public relations director.

I really worked hard to learn everything I could about the company, determined to know the electric-power business inside and out. I also became active in the National Electric Light

Association and was named chairman of its women's committee on public relations.

I'll never forget the day I was asked to speak at one of our conventions at Cedar Point. I went to the platform full of confidence, but without much speaking experience. Suddenly, while I was being introduced, my mind went blank. I had no idea what I was going to say. I panicked. Shakily I walked to the lectern. There was that awkward silence. Suddenly a voice inside told me, "Your Heavenly Father knows what you are going to say." "Well, take over then," I answered, and without hesitation I swung into my talk.

There were several things I wanted to talk about. Many of my teachers had been suffragettes, and I believed with all my heart that women were capable of more responsibility and should be given a chance. I told the mostly male audience that many of them had made the mistake of choosing "blue eyes over gray matter" when it came to their hiring practices. After my speech I got a big hand. It resulted in several more opportunities to speak, and before long I was going all over the country addressing various groups of businessmen.

One speech I'll never forget was one made to the American Electric Railways Convention in Washington. After my talk, I had my picture taken with President Coolidge and received the praise of B. C. Forbes, publisher of *Forbes* magazine. He said I should leave Lorain and come to New York where "there is so much more room for doing big things."

Though I didn't move my base of operations, I did form my own lecture bureau and my speaking assignments increased. One took me to Dayton in 1928 to address a group of bankers.

Afterward, a handsome young man named Franklin D. Rice, an officer with Dayton Savings and Trust, invited me to have dinner with him. I found him a wonderful person, warm and sensitive. We saw a lot of each other and within a year we were married.

The wedding was conducted by the Rev. Daniel Poling in New York City's historic Marble Collegiate Church. We honeymooned on a ship in the Caribbean and returned to a big house with Tiffany chandeliers and servants to polish them. Franklin was a prominent businessman, intelligent and wealthy. For my wedding present, he gave me a watch surrounded by one hundred diamonds. It was one big make-believe ball but, like Cinderella's, it was not to last.

Much of my husband's wealth was invested in stocks. During the great Depression, when the market crashed, he lost heavily. However, he did what wise investors do in bad times—he bought more. After all, he reasoned, the prices would look cheap when the market rebounded. But, of course, it didn't rebound—not until much, much later. Finally everything we owned was gone, and without any warning, so was Franklin. He had broken from the strain. A note he left me read, "Darling, the only thing I'm sorry about is that I never could give you all the things I meant to. . . . You'll always go on. I only knew one world. I just can't become a bum—I have to go out with the band playing."

It was like the shock that came with my father's death. I had no idea what I would do, if in fact I wanted to do anything. Then, out of the blue, the Gibson Greeting Card Company in Cincinnati asked me to come to work for them. "Make a survey of our cards and tell us how to improve them," the officers instructed me. I did as they said and came back with hundreds of recommendations. They accepted most of them, implemented them, and when the editor's job became vacant, I was appointed to fill it. That was in 1934.

For several years I edited the company's cards but did little writing. I created my own little greetings for friends, writing a verse on some special occasion, but those messages were not salable. According to the experts, my thoughts were too sentimental, too religious. In the 1950s, though, Gibson published some of my verses, offering them in a few markets with modest results.

Many people wrote me, however, and the spiritual help they received from the things I wrote greatly encouraged me. The response of people has always been my greatest reward. Then, in 1960, a performer named Aladdin read a verse I'd written called "The Priceless Gift of Christmas" on *The Lawrence Welk Show*. The response of the public was overwhelming. Thousands of people wrote to ask where they could find other poems like that one.

Since then God has opened a whole new world of friends to me. The simple verses I've written have been reproduced by the millions. They have been read on network TV and appeared in thousands of periodicals and dozens of books.

All I do is put down the words God places on my heart, and then he does the rest. He even finds the people who need to hear them. I'm the world's worst promoter of my verses. I leave the distribution of the words I put on paper to the Author, the One who inspires them.

"So where do you go from here?" someone asked me recently, knowing full well that I'm already beyond seventy years in age. My answer is, "One day at a time as he directs." I know that at my age, time is getting short. But I've faced what I thought was the end of the road before, and each time I've discovered what I wrote in this poem:

When we feel we have nothing left to give
And we are sure that the song has ended,
When our day seems over and the shadows fall
And the darkness of night has descended,
Where can we go to find the strength to valiantly
    keep on trying?
Where can we find the hand that will dry the tears
    that the heart is crying?
There's but one place to go and that is to God
And, dropping all pretense and pride,
We can pour out our problems without restraint
And gain strength with him at our side.
And together we stand at life's crossroads
And view what we think is the end;
But God has a much bigger vision,
And he tells us it's only a bend.
For the road goes on and is smoother
And the pause in the song is a rest,
And the part that's unsung and unfinished
Is the sweetest and richest and best.
So rest and relax and grow stronger;
Let go and let God share your load.
Your work is not finished or ended;
You've just come to a bend in the road.

His Mysterious Ways

IN THE EARLY 1970S, after at last acknowledging to myself that I was an alcoholic, I joined a group of admitted alcoholics who were dedicated to helping others achieve sobriety.

One night, at the close of the Tuesday meeting for newcomers, we got a call from the landlady of a transients' hotel in a part of town known as Wino Gulch. Would someone come talk to a man lying drunk in one of the rooms?

Two of us volunteered to go. When we reached the hotel we were led to a squalid little room where a grizzled oldster lay on the bed in a stupor. *What's the use of talking to this man at all?* I wondered. But my partner, an old hand at such visits, patiently talked to the semiconscious form on the bed. He explained that he himself had once been considered a hopeless drunk—but that by turning his life and will over to a Higher Power, he had gained both sobriety and serenity. "I'm leaving my card," my partner said. "I'd like you to attend a meeting at this address."

"That was a real waste of time," I grumbled as we departed.

"You never know," my partner said cheerfully. "God's always at work."

At our next meeting, a shaky but sober young man came up to us. "Thank you for coming to Wino Gulch that night," he said. "You saved my life."

We stared in astonishment. "We saw the old man on that bed very clearly," my partner said. "It wasn't you."

"That's right," the young man said, holding out the card we had left. "But I heard every word you said. I was under the bed."

—E.S., *November 1984*

Loving Life Enough

MARY MANACHI

February 1985

We'd just cut the watermelons at a Sunday school picnic, and I was laughing at the kids' antics—they were pretending to play harmonicas as they munched on the sweet pink slices, using the rind to make big green grins and seeing who could spit seeds the farthest. When I felt the woman's hand on my arm and saw her sympathetic, questioning eyes, I knew what she'd say before she even spoke.

"You seem so happy. Really happy. How do you do it after . . . after all that's happened to you?"

Again and again people ask me that same question—people who know that Louis and I had three children born with the blood disorder called Cooley's anemia. First Mary Lou, then Rosemary, then George. One after the other, they were born with it, lived with it, and died of it.

How can I be happy after all that's happened? Well . . .

Mary Lou was born in 1955. She was our second child, born

two years after our strong and healthy daughter, Ann. At first I'd thought Mary Lou's pale skin meant she took after my side of the family. Louis and I are both of Mediterranean descent, but he's the one with the olive complexion. When I took her to the pediatrician for her three-month checkup, he asked me to set up an appointment at a hospital in New York City for testing. "She seems to be anemic," he told me.

Anemia? It didn't sound too bad; lots of people have anemia. But after Mary Lou was tested at New York Hospital's Cornell Medical Center, the doctor called Louis and me in for a consultation.

"I'm sorry to have to tell you this," the doctor said. "Your baby has thalassemia major." He explained that this is commonly known as Cooley's anemia, after the doctor who discovered it. A rare genetic blood disorder, it prevents the body from manufacturing hemoglobin, the part of the red blood cells that carries oxygen from the lungs to body tissues and muscles.

"It mainly affects people of Mediterranean heritage," he told us. He also said that Cornell Medical Center was headquarters for the Harold Weill Clinic, which specializes in treating children with blood diseases. Mary Lou would have to go there every two weeks for a blood transfusion.

From then on I drove my small daughter into New York City from New Jersey regularly. After a few months she seemed to get used to it. And she had company; there were nineteen other children being treated for the same illness.

Louis and I wanted more children, but now we wondered.

"Don't worry," our doctor assured us. "It is very rare that this happens in a family twice."

Rosemary was born in 1959. She looked fine—bright blue eyes and fine brown hair like Mary Lou's. But just to be certain, I quickly took her to the clinic to be examined. The doctors were noncommittal. Weeks went by. One day she'd seem perfectly normal, the next her head would be sweating. The pattern had been the same with Mary Lou. Then, when Rosemary was six months old, the doctor gently told me that she would also need regular blood transfusions.

"Why didn't you tell me before?" I whispered. "Why did you let me hope?"

He shook his head sadly. "We knew how difficult it would be for you to hear this outright. We hoped you would recognize it gradually on your own."

So now I was driving two little girls into the city. It was easy to see how much Mary Lou and Rosemary depended on the transfusions. As the time for the treatments neared, they would tire easily and become irritable. But after their hospital visit—grueling as it was—they seemed fine. In the meantime, Louis and I tried to give our three daughters a normal life with music lessons, Monopoly games, and plenty of family outings.

In 1961 our son, George, was born. We had yearned for a boy, and we'd been assured that the chances of our having another child with the same affliction were absolutely nil.

But from the first moment I held my little boy in my arms, I knew. Deep down, I knew. Soon I was taking George into New York along with two-year-old Rosemary and six-year-old Mary Lou.

Even so, Louis and I were grateful for four lovely children. The blood transfusions simply became a regular part of our lives, and we went on hoping that a medical breakthrough would make them unnecessary. Meanwhile we were busy with the usual family things: school activities, music lessons, outings, and vacations. And the years passed.

Then came our shocking discovery.

One morning while I was waiting at the hospital, a mother of one of the other children quietly handed me a clipping from the *New York Times* headlined "Fatal Blood Disorder." It was about children coming to that very clinic. One sentence blazed out at me. "They usually die before they are twenty years old"

I couldn't believe it. I took the clipping to our doctor. "Is it true?" I asked.

"Yes," he sighed. "I'm afraid it is."

There were no drugs, no treatments, no known medical help to prevent my children's death at a young age.

For weeks Louis and I lived in a daze. His reaction was to say little and concentrate on his work as a garment designer. Mine was to cry whenever I was alone.

The children? We couldn't bring ourselves to discuss it with them, although I knew they were aware of the seriousness of their condition from talking with the other patients during their hospital visits. And then came one of those moments, small but significant, that changes the way you see things.

I had walked into eleven-year-old Rosemary's room one evening and found her making a jeweled butterfly pin. She was already selling her work at craft shows.

"How beautiful," I said, as I watched her carefully set a rhinestone.

"Thanks, Mom," she murmured. "I'm going to earn all I can toward college."

College? She was planning on college?

I cleared my throat. "Uh . . . what are you planning to study, hon?"

She looked up, eyes shining. "Nursing, Mom. I want to be like those nice women at the hospital who help me."

She turned back to her work and I walked slowly out of the room, trying to take it all in. Rosemary was not thinking about death; she was focusing on life.

At Thanksgiving one of her teachers phoned me. The class had been asked to write about what they were most thankful for. The answers were the usual ones about home, parents, and food. The teacher's voice trembled. "I thought you'd like to hear Rosemary's answer: 'I thank God for my good health.'"

Good health? How could she write that? And then I remembered the other children Rosemary saw on her hospital visits, the ones with amputations or suffering from cancer. But Rosemary could walk . . . go to school . . . skip rope.

Rosemary had filled our house with Scripture plaques that she made herself. In her own room she'd hung the one that said: "This is the day which the Lord has made; let us rejoice and be glad in it" (Psalm 118:24, RSV).

That Thanksgiving I looked around me. I saw that our house was not a house of shadows and sorrow: our children filled it with cheerfulness and bustling activity. Mary Lou's piano music rang through the rooms as she practiced for a recital. Rosemary busily crafted jewelry and wall plaques. Little George had an extensive rock collection; he was already talking about becoming a geologist. Slowly I began to see that my children, all of them, were rejoicing in life.

On July 4, 1969, Rosemary, then twelve, was in the hospital with a minor cardiac problem, a side effect of Cooley's. "You seem better, honey," I said to her that night as I leaned down to kiss her goodbye. "I'll be back early in the morning."

Just after I got home, the telephone rang. Rosemary was gone. "Peacefully," the hospital said.

We mourned. Mary Lou and George had known their lives would be short, but now, with Rosemary gone, they were forced to face that fact. Mary Lou, four years older than Rosemary, began carefully tending her sister's grave. I knew that she must be contemplating her own death. And yet, I watched carefully as she took up the business of her life with a new vitality. She began making the honor roll in high school and was very popular. And she made a suggestion that gave new direction to our lives.

Louis and I had been taking our children on more and more excursions, including a week's vacation in the Pennsylvania mountains. Soon after that trip, Mary Lou returned from her hospital visit in a thoughtful frame of mind.

"Mom," she said, "when I told the kids at the clinic about our visit to the Poconos, most of them said they'd never been to a place like that. Could we find a way to take them with us next time?"

"Of course we can," I said, hugging her. Suddenly we had a project. Right away I started organizing a volunteer group to take the other children on trips. We held bake sales and candy sales and raised enough money for an excursion to Mount Airy Lodge in the Poconos. Most of the children had never been together outside the hospital. How wonderful it was to see them laughing and having a good time away from the sting of needles, transfusions and spinal taps. We found ways to raise funds to see a Broadway play and even to visit Disney World.

In 1973 Mary Lou graduated from high school as a member of the National Honor Society. She had undergone surgery for removal of her spleen, so she had worked extra hard for these honors. In the fall, she entered William Paterson College as a fine-arts major. Soon she made the dean's list. She worked part time in a TV repair shop and her civic activities—everything from collecting for charity to volunteer work—put her in touch with almost everyone in town.

The following year she volunteered to participate in an experimental drug program for the treatment of Cooley's anemia. It took a lot out of her, and she had to be hospitalized for three weeks. "But if it helps other kids, it's worth it," she said.

Mary Lou was nineteen that Christmas of 1974. In January our Christmas tree was still standing in the living room. For some reason I just couldn't take it down.

On January 20th, it snowed heavily, keeping all of us at home. Mary Lou practiced her piano in the morning, but she was very tired. "I think I'll rest for a while," she said as she went up to bed. Later I brought her some lunch.

"Oh, this soup is so good!" she exclaimed. Then the light went out of her eyes and she fell back on her pillow.

Mary Lou's funeral was one of the largest ever seen in West Paterson. Louis and I had no idea that she had had so many friends. The mayor and the entire city council were there. In the words of the Cooley's volunteer group who honored her, she had been "A very special girl who lived and understood life better in her nineteen years than most of us could possibly hope to if we lived to be one hundred."

Later, as a cold February rain battered our living room window, I sat alone, thinking about this radiant daughter. Sighing, I leaned back, staring at the wall. In my line of sight were three of the Scripture plaques Rosemary had made for us. "I will never leave thee, nor forsake thee" (Hebrews 13:5). "Casting all your care upon him, for he careth for you" (1 Peter 5:7) "Do not be anxious about tomorrow" (Matthew 6:34, RSV).

The words wavered in my vision, then cleared. I got up immediately and began preparing dinner for my family.

Our oldest daughter Ann was involved in her career, and George, a typically noisy teenager, kept our house lively. His friends came and went and the telephone rang constantly. He dated and had an after-school job at a local restaurant. We continued to take the Cooley's children on trips and have get-togethers.

George graduated from high school and went on to Paterson College, where he threw himself into a full schedule of activities. He went on working part time at the restaurant, and the summer he was nineteen he bought a Chevrolet Monza sports car—shiny black with fire-engine-red trim. It was a young man's dream—and always full of his friends. He kept it in showroom shape.

On the night of September 20, I knew something was wrong. George came home from a date, and after he went to bed, I happened to notice that his Monza was pulled into the garage at a careless angle. Always before he'd aligned it so neat and straight.

The next morning he stayed home from school. "Mom," he said. "I just can't make it anymore. I'm so tired."

Louis and I took him for a long ride that night, knowing the moving car's hum and rhythm would help him doze off. When we got back to the house, he sank down on the couch. "I know I'm going, Mom," he said wearily. He looked up at me with concern. "Promise me you won't cry? You know where I'll be."

"No, Georgie, I won't cry."

My son smiled, shook his head, and lay back, eyes closed. Then he took a deep breath and was gone.

Mary Lou.

Rosemary.

George.

And so, again and again, people ask that question, "How can you be happy after all that's happened?"

I'll tell you how.

My children understood that life is a holy gift from our Creator. They loved each day they were given, and their enjoyment and gratitude were like sunlight, warming and brightening our time together. In the face of early death, they embraced life. If they loved life as much as they did, honoring it, reaching out to soothe their stricken friends, using their days creatively, am I to love life any less?

No! I will not dishonor God—or my children—with gloom and self-pity. I embrace life as they embraced it and I shall rejoice and be glad in it!

My Amazing Sheepskin Dream Coat

Joe Garagiola

December 1999

*Y*ou could always tell when Christmas was coming on "The Hill," the Italian-immigrant neighborhood in St. Louis where I grew up. The Nativity scene appeared on the lawn of the rectory at St. Ambrose, our church; and the other sure sign was the store windows. They looked a little fancier, with sprayed-on "snow" and the best items on display. It was there, in one of those windows the year I was ten, that I saw the greatest thing I'd ever laid eyes on.

A golden-brown sheepskin coat appeared in the window of Russo's Dry Goods. I'd take the long way home from school just to look at it and daydream about how it would feel buttoned around me. I wanted that coat more than anything, but I knew there was no way in the world I was ever going to get it.

Like most of the men in the neighborhood, my father

worked a long, tough day at Laclede-Christy, a clay-pipe factory. He stretched his paycheck to support our family and to pay the mortgage on our house. We always had food on the table, clothes to wear—I even had mine modeled for me by my big brother, Mickey, who wore them first—and a little to give to our church every week. But that didn't leave anything for luxuries such as a sheepskin coat.

One Sunday evening in early December, I stood in front of Russo's staring at the coat, taking in every detail as if there were something I might have missed all the other times I'd come to see it. The buttery brown leather. The fleece lining that looked almost golden in the right light. The cuffs, fitted so that on a windy day cold air wouldn't shoot up your arms. I pulled my thin cloth jacket a little higher around my neck. It didn't make me feel any warmer. Just the thought of that sheepskin coat did, though, and so close to Christmas, I couldn't think of anything else.

"You see that coat in Russo's window?" I asked as we sat down to dinner that night.

"That'll keep you warm, I guarantee you," said Uncle Tom, who lived with us. "Sheepskin, right?"

My mother set my favorite dish, risotto, on the table. For once I ignored it. "Yeah," I replied. "The coat looks plenty warm." I sneaked a glance at Pop. He smiled, but didn't say anything as he spooned a big helping of risotto onto my plate.

"Probably costs plenty too," Mickey laughed. "That coat would keep you warm even in a St. Louis winter!" We thought St. Louis was the coldest place on earth because we'd never been anywhere else.

"It'd sure be nice to have a coat like that," I hinted.

"It would be nice. A lot of things would be nice . . ." my father murmured, his thought trailing off like my hopes.

"Pop's right," I said to Mickey as we climbed into bed that night. "Lots of things would be nice, but I'm never gonna get 'em."

I wanted nice new things like other kids had. Not that any of those kids lived on The Hill. My friends got hand-me-downs too. We used cast-off baseball bats, fixing their cracks with nails. We taped up worn-out baseballs to get a few extra innings out of them. The guys who played catcher—I was one—made shin guards by stuffing old copies of *National Geographic* into our socks. Spikes were out of the question; Pop didn't believe in buying shoes you couldn't wear to church or school.

After wearing Uncle Tom's old shoes and Mickey's outgrown clothes for as long as I could remember, I dreamed of having something that was mine alone, something new. My father always taught me to dream big and never give up, so as Christmas got closer, I kept mentioning the sheepskin coat whenever he was within earshot. But he didn't say a word about it.

"What do you guess Pop is thinking?" I asked Mickey one night.

"What's he gonna say?" my brother answered impatiently. "If he told you, 'Forget about that sheepskin coat,' you'd be disappointed for weeks. If he doesn't say anything now, when you don't get it Christmas morning, you'll be disappointed for only a day."

I knew as well as Mickey did that our parents looked at Christmas as a holy day to honor our Lord's birth, not to give presents. We didn't even have a tree. Mickey and I would pull a kitchen chair beside our bed each Christmas Eve, and we'd wake up the next morning to find an orange on the seat, and maybe a shirt to wear to church. Our big holiday treat was panettone, an Italian fruitcake we ate only once a year.

With no word from Pop, I decided that if I was going to get my sheepskin coat, I'd have to ask somebody else: God. A few days before Christmas, I woke up before my brother and knelt by our bed. *I know I haven't been too good this year, God. But I promise, if you get me that coat, I'll do my best from now on.*

Christmas Eve night, Mickey and I set the chair beside our bed as usual. I don't remember how much I slept, but I sure remember waking up. I'll never forget waking up that morning.

There, draped over the chair, was my sheepskin coat from Russo's!

I jumped out of bed and got down on my knees. Rubbing my face in the golden fleece lining, I thought, *Thanks, God, you did a great job!* Then I threw the coat on—it felt so soft and warm, even better than I'd dreamed—and ran through the house, whooping and hollering.

Then I saw Pop standing in his bedroom doorway. Fat tears ran down his cheeks. I'd never seen my father cry. Still, I knew instinctively these were tears of happiness, like a safety valve on a full heart had opened, and I couldn't hold back my biggest smile.

I wore that sheepskin coat long past winter, late into spring. Good thing I had baseball to get me through the days until it was cool enough for me to put the coat on again. A couple of years later I finally outgrew it, and my mother passed it on to another kid who lived on The Hill.

There was something I got that Christmas I would never out-grow—something I didn't completely understand until the day I signed a contract at age sixteen to play baseball for the St. Louis Cardinals. I left Sportsman's Park with a five-hundred-dollar check, my signing bonus, in my hand. It was a hot, late summer afternoon, but I was so excited it might as well have been that Christmas morning all over again.

I took the Grand Avenue streetcar and headed for Laclede-Christy, where my father and the other men from The Hill were just sitting down with their lunch pails. Before Pop could ask what I was doing there, I pressed the check into his hand. He stared at it, then looked at me. Neither of us said anything. We didn't need to. We both knew the check would fulfill his dream of paying off the mortgage on our house. Watching Pop wipe his eyes and smile made me feel warm in a way no sheepskin coat ever could. I realized then that the joy of Christmas, and of the whole year through, is in giving as my father did—from the heart.

The Miracle of Laughter

August 2003

I knelt at the altar of the medieval church of St. Germain des Prés in Paris, the afternoon sun filtering through the stained-glass windows. Grace seemed to flow through that light. I experienced a profound sense of peace and holy intimacy. Finally, I rose and made my way toward the exit. I decided to stop in the bathroom before I rejoined my friends in a nearby café. When I was through, I dried my hands and pulled at the door. It didn't budge. I couldn't get out of the bathroom.

I peeked through a crack. Nuns and monks bustled back and forth. I rapped gently on the door. No response. I pounded. Harder. "Help!" I yelled. "I'm trapped." I heard mutterings outside, the sound of a key rattling in the lock. More commotion. Finally, with a mighty heave, a short, stout monk who looked like Friar Tuck fell through the doorway. "Madame," he gasped, catching his breath and leaning against the sink, "we have never had such excitement here."

EMBRACING THE JOYFUL LIFE
94

"I'm so sorry," I kept saying. I just wanted to get out of there as fast as I could. A little too fast, as it turned out. I tripped over a tourist's camera case and bumped into a stroller, causing the baby inside it to wail. By the time I reached the street, the church was in an uproar.

So much for my transcendent spiritual experience. And when it was all over, I couldn't stop laughing.

A lot of people think that our profound spiritual moments have to be serious—calming, centering, elegant. But is that really true? One Christmas Eve during a difficult time in my life, I found myself concentrating so intensely during the service that I gave myself a dreadful headache. The time for the Gospel reading arrived. The minister stood and read from Luke. He got to the part about the Baby Jesus wrapped in swaddling clothes and declared that the baby was "strapped in waddling clothes."

I couldn't help myself. I tried not to laugh; I really did. I buried my face in my hands. Maybe people thought I was in deep spiritual contemplation. Instead I was trying to compose myself and to stop thinking about "waddling clothes." By the time I finished giggling, my headache was gone. I felt clearer than I had in months. The minister's mistake made that Bethlehem manger feel even more grounded in reality; the heavenly and earthly were brought closer together. In the catharsis of my laughter I found peace.

Back in the fall of 1985, I was on assignment with my then-boss Norman Vincent Peale. Dr. Peale was to make a speech to a large gathering in a shopping mall near Washington, D.C. The Guideposts staff had worked on the event for months. TV news crews were coming from miles around to cover it. I had double-checked every detail, which was probably why I was feeling as tense as I was. I knew how much had to go right so that nothing went wrong. Sitting in the back seat of the car with Dr. Peale, I tried to hide my nervousness. In spite of all his experience speaking to crowds, I knew Dr. Peale got nervous too. *Please,* I prayed, *help us both relax and get through this.* Then I reassured myself that everything was going to be fine. I'd covered all my bases.

Except one. As we pulled into the mall parking lot, I spotted a marquee announcing the day's events. Norman Vincent Peale, it read in huge letters. And just beneath—Alfie the Cockatoo.

Oh, no, I thought. I glanced at Dr. Peale. He shot me a look back. And we both burst into laughter. "Never been on the bill with a bird before," Dr. Peale said—and once inside proceeded to deliver one of the most powerful talks I'd ever heard him give. He made sure that bird didn't upstage him. And I'd learned that you can worry yourself silly—yet silliness can make you relax and put everything into perspective.

"A merry heart doeth good like medicine," it says in Proverbs. And it's true. Take the Communion service at our church when a well-meaning parishioner mistakenly used a recipe for buttery shortbread instead of unleavened bread. Or the time my chair collapsed beneath me after singing Handel's *Hallelujah Chorus.* The Holy Spirit has a funny tendency to choose the most serious, intense, and even sacred moments to remind me to lighten up. Faith and laughter do go together, for me at least.

Last spring I was asked to speak at a big church outside

Atlanta. I love any reason to spend time with *Guideposts* readers; but just like Dr. Peale, I still get nervous about talking in front of a crowd. I walked from the parking lot and saw a poster announcing my event. The evening's speaker, it read, was the "hilarious" Mary Ann O'Roark. Me, hilarious? "Where did you get that idea?" I asked the woman who had invited me. "You sounded hilarious on the phone," she said.

The talk went well, maybe in part because it was a dress-up dinner, and one of the women in the audience wore a big red flamingo hat on her head that I couldn't take my eyes off. (Had she worn it in my goofy honor?) That word on the poster kept running through my mind. When I got home I took out my dictionary and looked up "hilarious." Its root: the Latin *hilaris*, meaning "cheerful."

Which brings me to one last story. As a little girl attending the United Presbyterian Church in Steubenville, Ohio, I heard grownups repeat a Bible verse that I was certain said, "God loveth a cheerful liver." I asked my grandma what a liver was. "It's a part inside you," she told me, "like your stomach or your heart." I puzzled over how to get my insides to be more cheerful. One day in Sunday school an older kid set me straight: "It's 'giver,' not 'liver.'" But I don't think I got it all that wrong. God does love a cheerful live-r. Living with *hilaritas*—cheer—is part of living abundantly. It's not just something it's okay for us to experience; it's something we're meant to do.

The Five Reasons
I Love My Life

DOLLY PARTON

July 2004

I hear it from folks all the time: "Gosh, Dolly, you seem so happy!" Well, my smile's pretty hard to miss, considering I'm a gal who likes her lipstick—the redder, the better. Take it from me, though, the fancy makeup is just highlighting what's for real. And that's true happiness, the kind that comes from the inside. Lately I've been giving it some thought, and I've come up with five things that make mine a happy life. Five things that make just about anyone's life joyous. Yours too, I bet.

1. *I love my friends and family.*
I grew up poor, so poor that my daddy paid the doctor who delivered me with a sack of cornmeal. Yet my family was rich in so many ways too. Each and every one of us twelve kids knew we were precious in the sight of God and cherished by our

mother and father. Maybe you've heard my song "Coat of Many Colors," about a girl who wears her coat of rags proudly. That came right out of my childhood in the Smoky Mountains in Tennessee. Someone gave us a box of rags, and Mama sewed them together to make a coat for me. The kids at school teased me, but I knew Mama put her love into every stitch. I felt proud to have that coat, and blessed.

Blessed as I felt the day I met Judy Ogle in third grade. My family had just moved to Caton's Chapel from another town in the Smoky Mountains. I walked into school, the new girl, too shy to make a peep. Until I noticed someone else quietly looking on. A girl with bright green eyes and a copper-colored ponytail. Something told me to go over and say hi.

Almost fifty years later, Judy and I haven't stopped talking. (Just ask my husband, Carl, who's always shaking his head at how we tie up the phone line.) If I get an idea for a tune while I'm picking at a guitar, Judy's there to write everything down before it goes out of my head. Whenever I need a dose of country air, Judy's there to drive out to the mountains with me. At the heart of every close friendship I have, there's what I discovered with Judy back in third grade—the magic of having someone in your life who understands where you're coming from and where you're going, who just knows.

2. *I love what I do.*

My daddy likes to say I was singing before I could talk. That might be a bit of a tall tale, but I can barely remember a time I wasn't making music. At age six, I was shaking the rafters at church. But our little country church could only fit so many people, and Sunday only came once a week. Mama said God had put his hand on me and given me my voice, so I decided he must have bigger plans for me.

Boy, did I want to be ready for them. I took up guitar at age seven, making my first instrument out of an old mandolin and two bass strings. I put on concerts right on our porch. To look the part of a glamorous singer, I used Mercurochrome for lipstick, crushed pokeberries for rouge and a burnt match for mascara. I'd collect my brothers and sisters who were too young to run away, sit them down in the dirt, then get up on the porch and belt out songs into a tin can on a stick like I was at the Grand Ole Opry. If I couldn't round up any of my brothers and sisters, there were always the pigs and chickens to serenade.

I landed my first professional gig on the Cas Walker Radio Show in Knoxville (I'll tell you all about it later). I was ten. I've been making a living doing what I love ever since. Is it any wonder that I feel incredibly fortunate? Not to mention grateful.

3. I love to laugh.

People often compliment my voice, my songwriting, my business acumen, and yes, my distinctive fashion sense. But I've always felt that my greatest gift is my positive attitude and sense of humor—they go together like biscuits and gravy. It's like the Bible says, "A merry heart doeth good like medicine." These past thirty-eight years with Carl have been one fun ride. He should hire himself out as a professional practical joker. I never know what he's going to pull next, but I do know it's going to leave me laughing.

I remember one concert in Louisville, Kentucky. My backup singers sounded kind of off. I glanced over my shoulder to see what was the matter. There was Carl at one of the microphones! And he had the audacity to wink at me. I decided to do him one better. I sauntered over to a policeman working security. "That man back there in the white shirt isn't part of our group," I told him. The cops hauled Carl away. It was all I could do not to crack up. (Don't worry, someone from our crew let the officers know who Carl was before they got too far.)

Having a live-in personal humor trainer like Carl is a big help. There are things I do on my own too, to keep my attitude in shape. I close my eyes and picture angels surrounding me. I tell them whatever's troubling me, then I envision them trampling those burdens to powder. If my attitude needs more adjusting, I visualize God holding me upside down and shaking all the negative stuff—fears, doubts, insecurities— right out of me. Try it. Ask God to turn you upside down! It's a sure-fire pick-me-up.

4. *I love to pray.*

Getting up close and personal with God is something I learned in his house. Not the way you'd expect, though. I used to explore the old church my town, Caton's Chapel, was named after. It was a ruin—shattered windows, buckled floor, graffiti-splattered walls. Saturday nights, teenagers partied there. Mama was aware of the not-so wholesome goings-on and warned us to steer clear of the place. But for some reason I was drawn to it, during daylight hours anyway. I'd hunt for doodlebugs in the cool earth under the floorboards or daydream at the broken piano in the corner.

And I'd pray. I would tell God how I wanted to see the world that lay beyond the Smoky Mountains. To make it as a country music star and have a whole building full of folks to sing to. To do Mama and Daddy proud.

Was God listening? I couldn't quite tell. Then one day I was sitting in a pew, talking to him, when suddenly something changed in the very air around me. Something changed inside me too. I felt like I would bust with happiness. God was right there with me. I was absolutely sure. I didn't have to jump up and down or shout or even sing to get his attention. I could just whisper. He heard every word. Something I would have done well to remember in the early 1980s, when I was going through the darkest time. Not that I had any real reason to be unhappy. I had a strong marriage, tons of family and friends, a well-established career. But a movie I'd made hadn't turned out well. I had some serious medical issues. Judy was going through a crisis of her own, so I couldn't lean on her like usual. And poor Carl was so worried about my health that I didn't want to put any more on him. For the first time in my life, I felt all alone. Like no one was listening, not even God.

It was more an act of desperation than inspiration, but I grabbed for the only lifeline I could think of. The Bible. I sat down and read it cover to cover, a little every day. Pretty soon verses jumped out at me. Like that line in 1 Thessalonians that always had me stumped: "Pray without ceasing." How on earth was I going to do that? Coming out of that dark time, that's when I finally got what those words meant. No matter where I go or what I'm doing, a part of me is talking to God. And a part of God is listening.

5. *I love you.*

I believe God put the dream in my heart to become a country music performer so I could share the love he poured into my life with as many people as possible. I know you might think, *that's just Dolly being outrageous again,* but why else would God have let me discover what I did the first time I sang in front of an audience?

This gets back to that first gig I mentioned. I landed it thanks to my uncle, Bill Owens. I was ten, and he took me to Knoxville to meet Cas Walker, the host of a live music radio show. Cas said hello and stared down at me like he expected me to say something back. Well, I did. I said, "Mr. Walker, I want to work for you." He shook my hand and said, "You're hired. A lot of people come to me and say, 'Mr. Walker, I want a job,' but you're the first one that ever said, 'I want to work.'"

The show was recorded in an auditorium that seated about sixty people. I walked up to the microphone and looked out at the audience. All those strangers! Whoa, this was a whole lot different from getting up in front of the pigs and chickens on our farm. The first notes were kinda squeaky. Pretty soon, though, the sheer joy of singing took over.

I finished with a flourish. Everyone clapped and stomped their feet. They wanted an encore, but I didn't have one. I looked over at Uncle Bill, and he mouthed. "Sing it again." So I did—and they cheered all over again, even louder. I never knew I could feel so close, so connected, to a bunch of strangers. That was the moment I fell in love with the people I sing for. With you. I've loved y'all ever since.

I am a happy person. That is my greatest blessing. It can be yours too. Think about it. Friends and family, work, laughter, prayer, love. They add up to joy. For you, for me, for anyone.

Facing Life's Challenges

Her Final Gift

NATALIE KALMUS

September 1947

on't worry, but come as soon as you can," my sister, Eleanor Smith, wired. At the time, I was in London working out problems with one of the British motion picture companies.

I felt a deep, numbing pang. I knew Eleanor had been ill for some time. Surely this was her gentle way of telling me that the end was coming.

I could not accept it. Always radiating charm, friendliness, and an inner happiness, my sister had been a wonderful inspiration to those close to her. She had that rare trait of always giving others a pat on the back—lifting their spirits and sending them off with a fresh outlook on life.

When she was first stricken by the most fearsome of medical enemies, the doctors had told her that her days were numbered. Knowing this had not made the slightest difference in her warm interest in people—nor in her deep abiding faith in the wonder of God.

But now she needed me. I returned to the States and hurried to Eleanor, expecting to find her in bed in great pain. Instead she was in the living room perched jauntily on the sofa, looking more like a schoolgirl of seventeen than an incurably ill woman.

"Natalie," she held out her arms joyously. "I'm so happy now that you're here. We have so much to talk over." To anyone listening I might have dropped in for a casual call.

After Eleanor had retired for the night, the doctor drew me aside. "Mrs. Kalmus," he said, "I think that it will be a most trying experience for you if you stay here through to the end. I'm afraid that your sister's last hours will be an agony of pain."

Medically, I knew he was right. Yet the radiance I noticed in my sister's face seemed somehow to refute his statement. The strange feeling swept over me that the strength of my sister's spirit could well triumph over her pain.

During the next few days, I discovered that Eleanor was doing many things that baffled the doctors. They were preparing her for some grim final moments. She was ignoring their solemn suggestions and remedies. One night she had me sit down on the side of her bed.

"Natalie, promise me that you won't let them give me any drugs. I realize that they are trying to help relieve my pain, but I want to be fully aware of every sensation. I am convinced that death will be a beautiful experience."

I promised. Alone later, I wept, thinking of her courage. Then, as I tossed in bed through the night, I realized that what I took to be a calamity, my sister intended to be a triumph.

One afternoon Eleanor, in the most airy and lighthearted

manner, asked several friends to a dinner party that she decided to hold on the spur of the moment. I was stunned. But Eleanor grinned at me impishly, in high spirits. The sight of the happiness in her face checked my objections.

On the night of the party, Eleanor dressed meticulously, concealing the pain I knew she felt. We helped her downstairs before the guests were to arrive. Sitting in a turquoise chair in her yellow evening gown, she sparkled with life and gaiety.

The party was a grand success; the guests were never once aware of the illness that my sister concealed so expertly. That night, however, when she was carried to bed, her deep physical weariness appeared on the surface. I realized then that my sister knew this was her final social fling. She had planned it that way.

Days later the final hour drew near. I had been at her bedside for hours. We had talked about many things, and I marveled at her quiet, sincere confidence in eternal life. Not once did the physical torture overcome her spiritual strength.

"Dear kind God, keep my mind clear and give me peace," she had murmured over and over again during those last days.

We had talked so long that I noticed she was drifting off to sleep. I left her quietly with the nurse and retired to get some rest. A few minutes later I heard my sister's voice calling for me. Quickly I returned to her room. She was dying.

I sat on her bed and took her hand. It was on fire. Then she seemed to rise up in bed almost to a sitting position.

"Natalie," she said, "There are so many of them. There's Fred . . . and Ruth—what's she doing here? Oh, I know!"

An electric shock went through me. Ruth! Her cousin Ruth

had died suddenly the week before. But Eleanor had not been told of Ruth's death.

Chill after chill shot up and down my spine. I felt as if I were on the verge of some powerful, almost frightening knowledge.

Her voice was surprisingly clear. "It's so confusing. So many of them!" Suddenly her arms stretched out as happily as when she had welcomed me! "I'm going up," she murmured.

Then she dropped her arms around my neck and relaxed in my arms. The will of her spirit had turned her final agony into rapture. As I laid her head back on the pillow, there was a warm, peaceful smile on her face.

This was my sister's inheritance to me—her final, beautiful gift. I had seen for myself how thin was the curtain between life and death. I had glimpsed part of the wonderful truth about everlasting life. Never again will death frighten me in any way.

His Mysterious Ways

"THE LORD sustains him on his sickbed . . ." (Psalm 41:3, RSV).

I was suffering one of my worst asthma attacks. It was so bad that Mom took me to the hospital, where a doctor gave me a shot. "This is about the best we can do for you," he said. "If you're having problems in the morning, come back immediately."

That night I asked my parents to set up a bed for me on the living room couch. I didn't want to keep my brother up; I was wheezing and gasping for breath.

For a long while I tossed and turned. I didn't have the strength to get out of bed, so I lay there, listening to the sounds of the night, praying for relief. At last a time came when my breathing eased and I drifted off to sleep.

When I woke up, Mom was leaning over me, smiling. "Barry, how do you feel?"

"Fine," I said, breathing deeply. "No problem." Then I noticed a chair that had been pulled close to the couch as if someone had been sitting there. "Did you or Dad come in after I went to sleep?" I asked.

"No," Mom said, "we listened, but you seemed to be better."

"But when did you move the chair next to me?"

"Why, Barry," she said, "we didn't."

"I didn't either!" I exclaimed. "I couldn't have moved last night if I had tried."

And then I remembered the feeling I'd had as I dozed off. Someone—yes, Someone— was sitting at my side.

—BARRY RUDESILL, *October 1990*

Do It Scared!

Linda Neukrug

June 1990

A nyone who reads the paper knows that at 5:04 P.M. October 17, 1989, northern California suffered a terrible earthquake. Anyone who knows me knows that I am not the kind of person who would do anything heroic. Yet oddly enough, something happened to me during the quake that changed my life.

It all began when I was sitting at my word processor at my job in San Francisco, on the top floor of a very old brick building. What I was doing was rehearsing.

"Excuse me, Gerald. Is now a good time to talk to you about my raise?" Too wishy-washy.

"Gerald, I must talk to you about my raise. It's way overdue," Too pushy.

I sighed and put the plastic cover on my word processor. It was 5:00 P.M., and another day had gone by without my bringing up the subject of the year-and-a-half delay in my getting a raise. I knew I deserved this raise. I had a feeling that Gerald knew it too. Maybe he'd just forgotten. He'd been so busy lately. Maybe, in fact, he'd call me in about it tomorrow and . . .

There I was, off in fantasyland again. I'd been thinking that wishful scenario for over two months. The one time I'd approached Gerald, I'd gotten as far as saying his name before my voice had gone all quavery, and I'd finished by saying, "We need more paper clips." Then I'd made a breathless escape and never brought up the subject again.

That pattern was nothing new for me; it was what I always did when afraid. I'd pray to God a few times to remove my fears, but if nothing happened, I'd figure it wasn't that important and move on to something else. It seemed to make sense, and yet I always seemed to live with an undercurrent of fear. There are so many things I just avoid doing. Like asking for that raise. Like walking down those stairs.

Those stairs! I work in an old brick building that is being gutted for renovation. Every day, scores of workers in hard hats come in and drill and jackhammer and demolish walls. There is yelling and noise and dust flying everywhere. Broken concrete and wires lie around. Most of the time there are no lights. Architects and engineers swarm through, all armed with blueprints, talking about sconces and rebars and demo dust. I have to wear a hard hat just to be allowed in the building (and I'm a typist!).

Worse, the elevator was so slow and creaky that I was afraid to take it after I briefly got stuck once. So I tried the stairs. What a mistake! They were rickety and made of plywood, and they were strewn with dust, debris, candy wrappers, and coils of rope. They were covered with about an inch of dust and booby-trapped (in my opinion) with wooden scaffolding and metal. Every time I bent to duck under the scaffolding, my hard hat would fall, and I'd lunge for it. I'd lost my footing once and vowed then that I would never take the stairs again. And I hadn't.

Pulling on my coat, I thought about how fear ruled my life. Prayer didn't seem to help. After all, I'd asked God many times to remove my numerous fears, but I was still as fearful as ever. Now I poked my head into my boss's office: "Goodnight, Gerald. I'll see you tomor—"

The wooden floor started swaying.

I looked at him, he looked at me, and at the same moment, we both said, "Earthquake!" Automatically, I jumped under a doorjamb, just like I'd seen people do on TV. I think he went under his desk. I don't know because the power went off, and we were left in darkness while the building shook.

From down the hall, a calm voice said clearly, "I will not be shaken." (I later found out that was from Psalm 16: 8, NIV.) Another voice screamed, "Evacuate! Evacuate! Evacuate the building!"

I responded to that second voice. Out of habit, I made for the elevator, then stopped. How ridiculous! There was no power, so of course, no elevator! I'd have to walk downstairs. When that realization hit, I froze. A long line of people walked by the office. I couldn't see who they were, but I followed.

I was next to last in line. I tried to be last, but there were two people who'd apparently been trained in emergency prepared-ness. One had taken the front of the line, and one the end. So I marched along, terrified, until I stopped suddenly at the head of the stairs. The actual earthquake was over, but the building was still shaking. And I, of course, was still shaking too! There I stood, at the top of those rickety stairs. Again I could hear that woman's calm voice: "I will not be shaken."

Well, I was shaken! The feeling I had was the feeling you are familiar with if you have ever stood at the edge of a diving board, about to jump, or if you have ever gone skydiving and it is your turn to leave the plane next. (Not that I have done either of these things! But I imagine the feeling is similar—that feeling of being about to step into nothingness when you don't think anything will be there after you take that step.)

"Walk!" the lady behind me insisted.

"I can't!" I cried.

"Do it!" Her voice was commanding.

"I'm scared!" I wailed. "I can't do it if I'm scared!"

"Then say, 'I will not be shaken,' and do it scared!"

Do it scared! To my amazement, my feet started moving. One step, then another, and another . . . one floor, then another . . . The wall at each level had been spray-painted with a huge numeral, so as I made it down to each floor . . . 8 . . . 7 . . . 6 . . . I seemed to hear the words *Do it scared!* reverberating in my head. . . . 5 . . . 4 . . . 3 . . .

I had been going about it all wrong! I had been waiting for the fear to leave before I attempted something that frightened me. I'd never even thought of doing something while scared.

By the time I got to the second floor, the walk downstairs seemed routine. And then . . . freedom! I walked outside into the daylight and into crowds of people milling around, talking about the earthquake.

We couldn't get into the building for two days. When we were allowed back in, I decided to speak to Gerald. Immediately, my heart pounded and my stomach felt queasy. *I'm scared,* that little yapping voice in my head said. *It'll be easier tomorrow.*

"I will not be shaken," I firmly told that voice. Then I told myself, "So you're scared? Then do it scared!"

So I went right up to Gerald, my knees knocking, my palms damp, and said, "Gerald, I need to talk to you about my raise."

The Code

GERALD COFFEE

August 1990

The dismal echo of the door to my new cell clanging shut merged with the sharp slap of the guard's sandals as he made his way with short, rapid steps out of the cellblock. I heard the thud of another door shut and lock, then another, each one distantly punctuating my sense of desolation. Finally all that was left was silence, the harsh, pounding silence I'd endured for four long months of solitary captivity since being shot down on a Navy reconnaissance mission over North Vietnam in February 1966. Silence like I had never known before. Silence I'd futilely tried to fill with thoughts of home, my wife, my bed, and our children back in California; of other captured U.S. airmen I knew must be here, somewhere, confined in the grim reaches of Hanoi's Hod Lo prison.

Isolated, desperately alone, I was in a strange, faraway place where I was the enemy. I'd had only two fleeting encounters with other American POWs. The first was with Colonel Robinson Risner after I'd heard him softly whistling "Yankee Doodle" in the courtyard outside my original cell. He identified himself as senior officer at Hod Lo. Quickly the guards had approached—and that was the last I saw of Risner. Then, late one night I heard them dump a badly injured pilot in the next cell. He moaned and wept deliriously as I pounded the wall. "Hang on!" I shouted. At dawn his voice had faded, and his breathing stopped with a heaving, rattling sigh. Later I caught the stench of bleach as the guards sluiced out the cell. The pilot had probably bled to death. A raw fury built within me. Kneeling in a fading slash of morning sunlight, I prayed for him—and for my own survival.

Then there was that letter I'd written.

When "Rabbit," a young Vietnamese officer, had offered me the chance to write home, I'd been secretly elated, but suspicious. I'd learned my captors never gave anything away. "But Co," he'd said, smiling reproachfully as he used the odd Vietnamese shorthand for my name, "do you not wish to inform your loved ones in America that you are safe?"

When I'd finished, Rabbit looked the letter over. "But wait," he remarked smoothly, arching his brow and feigning offense, "what about our humane and lenient treatment?"

My foot, I grunted to myself. It'd taken over a month to set my fractured right arm. Now that the grotesque swelling had subsided, the cast rattled around loosely like a giant bracelet; I'd stuffed paper and rags down it to keep the bone rigid. Still, I scrawled out another laborious, left-handed draft, including the bit about humane and lenient treatment. Bea will see right through it, I figured.

"But Co," clucked Rabbit this time, tossing his head like an imperious schoolmaster, "there is nothing here of your black-hearted imperialist crimes against my people."

"I refuse," I shot back, slapping down the pencil stub. "I'd rather not write."

Rabbit's face reddened. He flew out of his chair and tore the letter to pieces as the guards hauled me back to my cell, where they flung me in a heap and administered a few blunt kicks to my ribs for good measure.

At midnight that night I was awakened by my cell door being jarred open. For the first time I glimpsed the ominous ropes and heavy iron bar with which I was soon to become so familiar, and it was in the hours near dawn, after they'd dislocated my shoulder and my hips, that I heard myself sobbing through the violence and pain, "I'll write it! I'll write it! Oh, God, please let me write it!"

A month later, I was still punishing myself for my weakness. If only I had someone to talk to, maybe I could shake this beast of shame. I glanced around my new quarters and wondered what part of the prison they'd moved me to this time. Like all the others, this cell fairly reeked of human misery. A dim, grimy light bulb dangled from the ceiling, and a discolored slab of concrete served as a bed. At the end of the cell were ankle stocks and a roughly formed manacle. Lengthwise the cell could be spanned with three shuffling steps. I noticed some bloodied scraps of bandage in the shadows, and I reclaimed them from the rat that was gnawing on them, shoving them down my frayed cast for support.

And there, carefully etched in the wall, was the ever-present diagram, a neat little grid of letters and numerals. Since my first day I'd noticed them everywhere throughout the prison. Obviously they were put there by English-speakers. But why? What strange things to see in a North Vietnamese jail. I couldn't figure them out.

I eased myself onto the slab, trying to protect my arm, and wondered what had happened to Risner and the others. It was siesta time for the Vietnamese. As I drifted off into a half-dream about a Fourth of July picnic back home in Modesto, a sharp, distant whisper pierced my reverie: "Man in cell six with the broken arm, listen up!"

Was I delirious? I shot up and cocked an ear.

"New man, can you hear?"

That voice. It was Risner's! "I hear you, Colonel. It's me, Lieutenant Coffee." The words sprang from my lips. The unfamiliarity of my own voice startled me.

"Welcome to Heartbreak Hotel, Jerry. Try not to talk so loud. Communication is forbidden. The man in cell one is clearing for us by watching under his door for the guard's shadow. If you hear a single cough or thump on the wall, stop talking immediately."

"Sir, how many of you are . . ."

"About forty in Heartbreak. Listen, Jerry, talking is very dangerous. You must learn to communicate by tapping on the walls. It's called tap code.

"The code is the only link we have," Risner continued. "Look for a square of letters comprising the alphabet—except we use 'c' for 'k'—and numerals running along the top and one side. To get the letter you want, simply tap the number of the row, then the number of the column."

So that was what those maddening little diagrams were all about.

Cough. Thump.

Risner stopped in mid-whisper. I heard the door at the end of the cellblock rattle open and the guard shuffle in. I could sense his suspicion through the dimness of the passageway. There would be no more talk today.

But I was ecstatic to finally be in touch with the others. It was as if I'd tumbled out of a long, black tunnel. Over the next few days we had sufficient clearing for me to become adept with the code. I told of events back home. Men in other cells tapped in and out of the "conversation," eager to know who had won the World Series or what politicians were saying about the war. One thing still haunted me, though—that letter. Finally I told Risner.

"Jerry," he tapped back, "we have all been made to do things here against our will. The folks back home can see through the propaganda. All the Code of Conduct asks is that you resist to your utmost, make them fight you for what they get, and give them as little as possible. You fought."

"But I can't forgive myself," I tapped.

"You must. It's how we recover that counts. That's how we get back at them. Remember, no matter what they do to us, we have the code. We have one another. None of us could have made it this long otherwise."

Day-to-day survival, I found, depended on the code. We'd spill a little water under our doors in the morning; the reflection would alert us to an approaching guard. A crude alarm system was devised by dropping bits of rice to attract the rats; they'd squeal off at the first sign of trouble. When we couldn't use the walls, we'd signal by coughing, or flashing our fingers, or tapping our feet. In the worst of times, we'd yank threads from our clothes and tie tiny knots that corresponded with the code. The nature of the code forced us to be direct and honest. We'd argue, we'd commiserate, we'd comfort, we'd joke, we'd tease, we'd tap out hymns, and we'd pray. Always we prayed through those grim walls; we prayed for strength, for hope, for our families back home, but mostly for one another.

Nothing infuriated our captors more than to discover we'd been transmitting messages, especially to men in solitary like Robbie—Colonel Risner—who had spent years in isolation and months in total darkness. They were not sophisticated enough to stop us—and nothing could have—but Rabbit would undertake periodic campaigns to break us. Then the torture would start as they tried to find out about our communication methods, our chain of command, who was telling whom what. We did our best to resist, and some men died from the brutality. Nothing was more anguishing, not even the hated ropes themselves, than to be carried back to your cell after a session and have to tell a man that you implicated him in some way in the communication network. It sometimes happened, and we understood. We forgave. As long as you made them fight you for it. It's all we asked of one another.

One night a man was brought back after a couple of days' absence. I'll call him Eddie. I could tell by his grunts and moans as they heaved him on his slab that he'd been through it. I immediately tapped in: "Welcome home, Eddie." There was no answer. I tapped again. Still no response. I tried for hours. I didn't want to lose him. "Stay with me, fella," I tapped. Then, late into the night, he tapped back weakly: "I'm so sorry, Jerry. They wanted names. I gave them yours."

My name. I didn't know what to say. I didn't know if I could stand the ropes another time, the agony of torn muscle and cartilage, of twisted limbs. I'd be next, and nothing was worse than waiting for it.

Eddie kept tapping "I'm sorry," over and over. But I was thinking about faith. And about the code. What is this inextinguishable need we humans have to communicate, to reach out and be reached, to share faith? If there is one thing Hoa Lo had taught me it is that faith is never a more powerful instrument of survival than when it is shared.

Finally, urgently, forcefully, I tapped back, "Thou preparest a table for me in the presence of my enemies." A minute later Eddie responded, his tapping now stronger, more confident, "Even though I walk through the valley of the shadow of death, I fear no evil."

They came for me at dawn. Eddie switched from tapping to coughing Psalm 23. Others were able to signal too. I tried to tear my mind away from reality. I thought about Bea and the children, and dredged the backwaters of my memory to summon up the kindest moments of my life to cling to. I could feel the strength of the others reaching through the dimness, and I knew that when I returned, numb and battered, my brothers in the cellblock would be checking under their doors to see if it was safe to start tapping out support, to gather close and bring me back with love and prayer from the abyss we had all faced.

It would be seven years before I'd taste freedom, seven bleak years of uncertainty. There were times I thought I couldn't hold on any longer. Then those gorgeous, curious little diagrams I'd puzzled over for so long saved me.

Thinking back on my years in Heartbreak Hotel, I am reminded that human communication is a never-ending source of comfort and strength. Through the dark, impenetrable prison walls of Hoa Lo, the code kept us in touch with our faith and with one another. It kept us alive.

The Last Tape

NAN PINKSTON

July 1997

he bustle of the hospital was a welcome distraction as I opened my new patient's chart and headed for her room. My son, Eric, had just brought home a disappointing report card, and my daughter, Shannon, and I had argued again about her getting a driver's license. For the next eight hours, I wanted to throw myself into helping people who I knew had much more to worry about than I did.

Rebekah was only thirty-two, admitted for chemotherapy after breast-cancer surgery. When I entered her room, it took me a moment to spot her amid the bouncing forms of three giggling little girls.

I told Rebekah I would be her nurse, and she introduced her husband, Warren; six-year-old Ruthie; four-year-old Hannah; and two-year-old Molly. Warren coaxed the girls away from their mother with a promise of ice cream and assured Rebekah they would return the next day.

As I rubbed alcohol on her arm to prepare it for the intravenous line, Rebekah laughed nervously. "I have to tell you that I'm terrified of needles."

"It'll be over before you know it," I said. "I'll give you a count of three."

Rebekah shut her eyes tightly and murmured a prayer until it was over. Then she smiled and squeezed my hand. "Before you go, could you get my Bible from the table?" I handed her the worn book. "Do you have a favorite Bible verse?" she asked.

"'Jesus wept.' John 11:35."

"Such a sad one," she said. "Why?"

"It makes me feel closer to Jesus, knowing he also experienced human sorrow."

Rebekah nodded thoughtfully and started flipping through her Bible as I shut the door quietly behind me.

During the following months I watched Rebekah struggle with the ravages of chemotherapy. Her hospital stays became frequent, and she worried about her children. Meanwhile I continued to contend with raising my own kids. They always seemed either to be out or holed up in their rooms. I missed the days when they were as attached to me as Rebekah's little girls were to her.

For a time it had seemed Rebekah's chemotherapy was working. Then doctors discovered another malignant lump. Two months later, a chest X-ray revealed that the cancer had spread to her lungs. It was terminal. *Help me to help her through this,* I prayed.

One day when I entered her room, I found her talking into a tape recorder. She picked up a yellow legal pad and held it out to me. "I'm making a tape for my daughters," she said.

I read the list on her pad: starting school, confirmation, turning sixteen, first date, graduation. While I worried about how to help her deal with death, she was planning for her children's future.

Rebekah usually waited until the early hours of the morning to record the tapes, so she could be free from interruptions. She filled them with family stories and advice—trying to cram a lifetime of love into a few precious hours. Finally, every item in her notes had been checked off, and she entrusted the tapes to her husband.

I often wondered what I would say in her place. My kids joked that I was like an FBI agent with my constant questions about where they'd been and who they'd been with. *Where,* I thought, *are my words of encouragement and love?*

It was three o'clock one afternoon when I got an urgent call from the hospital. Rebekah wanted me to come immediately with a blank tape. *What topic has she forgotten?* I wondered.

She was flushed and breathing hard when I entered her room. I slipped the tape into the recorder and held the microphone to her lips. "Ruthie, Hannah, Molly—this is the most important tape." She held my hand and closed her eyes. "Someday your daddy will bring home a new mommy. Please make her feel special. Show her how to take care of you. Ruthie, honey, help her get your Brownie uniform ready each Tuesday. Hannah, tell her you don't want meat sauce on your spaghetti. She won't know you like it separate. Molly, don't get mad if there's no apple juice. Drink something else. It's okay to be sad, sweeties. Jesus cried too. He knows about sadness and will help you to be happy again. Remember, I'll always love you."

I shut off the recorder and Rebekah sighed deeply. "Thank you, Nan," she said with a weak smile. "You'll give this one to them, won't you?" she murmured as she slid into sleep.

The time would come when the tape would be played for Rebekah's children, but right then, after I smoothed Rebekah's blanket, I got in my car and hurried home. I thought of how my Shannon also liked her sauce on the side, and suddenly that quirk, that had annoyed me so many times, seemed to make her so much more precious. That night the kids didn't go out; they sat with me long after the spaghetti sauce had dried onto the dishes. And we talked—without interrogations, without complaints—late into the night.

Nine Men Safe

ROB ZAREMSKI

November 2002

he news blared from my car radio that muggy day last July. "Nine miners are still trapped in the flooded Quecreek coal mine in Somerset, Pennsylvania, at this hour. . . ." I was 150 miles away from Somerset, driving east on I-80 to make a sales call. With emerald-green trees rushing past on either side of the highway and the hazy outline of mountains in the distance, it was tough for me to imagine the gritty darkness those miners were stuck in, so far from help and home. Almost reflexively, I said a quick prayer for their safety.

I'd been praying a lot lately. Though my own problems paled in comparison to the miners', they'd kept me up more than a few nights lately. I'd taken a new job as a sales rep with Targeting Customer Safety selling industrial safety and rescue equipment. I'd been in the industry for years, but now it was as bad a market as I could remember. I was under a lot of pressure and sometimes I felt as if I were all on my own. My wife, Colleen, was always telling me not to worry. But with her and our three kids, Caylin, Isaac, and Megan, to support, I couldn't afford to fail. Though I knew God was watching out for us, I couldn't really expect him to make sure I hit my numbers, could I? That was up to me. My car already had more than two hundred thousand miles on it, and each day added more, as I followed up on even the slimmest of prospects.

I turned down the radio when my cell phone rang. It was Denny Swigert, the co-owner of my company. "Rob, drop what you're doing," he said. His voice was tense. "I just got a call. The guys trying to rescue those trapped miners need a communications probe and nine hundred feet of wire ASAP."

I was stunned. Only a moment before, the miner rescue was a news story on the radio. Now it was personal. The probe was a fairly new device and had been used in search-and-rescue efforts after last year's terrorist attacks. It sort of looks like a stainless steel hot dog with little holes in it. Lowered on a communications cable, it can pick up and transmit sounds without a lot of background noise.

"Meet me in Warren," Denny continued. "The fire department there has what we need." I cancelled my sales call and met Denny to pick up the equipment, then I sped to Somerset. State troopers got word of my mission and waved me on. My leg grew stiff as I pressed steadily on the accelerator, hoping my old car would hold out. "C'mon, you can do it!" I muttered. Those guys needed all the help they could get—and fast.

I wasn't sure what I could do once I got there though. I wasn't a rescue worker. I knew the equipment backward and forward, but my involvement usually ended with praying that each piece I sold would protect and aid the customer.

The Quecreek mine area was a mass of drilling machinery, air compressors and somber-faced rescue workers. I learned that the trapped miners had broken through a wall of the forgotten Saxman mine while forging into what they thought was a thick seam of coal. They barely had a chance to radio nine other nearby miners to get out before sixty million gallons of water crashed over them.

Now a giant drill was boring a thirty-two-inch-wide rescue shaft. Close by was a six-inch pilot hole through which hot air was being pumped to keep the miners alive and to build pressure to stop the floodwaters from rising higher. Tapping sounds had come from the hole earlier. But not anymore. Were the men still alive? Had the water risen too high?

There was nothing to do but wait until there was a suitable spot to try out the probe. I got a motel room for the night and called my wife to tell her about my change in plans.

"I've been watching the news coverage all day," said Colleen. "I'm so glad you're there trying to help. Everyone's praying for those men."

Lying in bed that night, I thought of those guys deep underground. They were probably wondering if they'd ever again get to kiss their wives goodbye in the morning or tuck their children in at night. So many people, so many prayers, but how would we reach the men? All the equipment we had, all the technology, and still we were in doubt. I tossed and turned till four o'clock in the morning, then headed back to the site.

Cows grazed sleepily just outside the glare of the floodlights illuminating the rescue site. One of the rescue supervisors, Jeff Kravitz, took me to another six-inch hole, which led down into the old Saxman mine, about four hundred yards from where they thought the miners were. But Jeff said there was a cushion of a few feet between the water and the ceiling through which sound might travel to the men.

"The drill bit just broke about one hundred feet down," Jeff said. "They're starting another shaft while they try to get the broken bit out of the first hole. But it's going to take time. I hate to think of them down there hearing that drill stop. It's a long shot, but if there's any chance to get through to them, to keep them going, we've got to try."

The hole was actually in the backyard of the Stanczyks, a kindly middle-aged couple who had told the rescue workers to do whatever it took to help the miners, even if it meant bulldozing their house. They offered me coffee and food, and then I got down to business. I put on my headset and lowered the probe into the hole. A small crowd surrounded me expectantly. I spoke the standard message officials had told me to say. "Stay where you are, tap ten times and the rescue team will pick up your signal."

No response. I repeated the message. Nothing. One by one people around me wandered back to the drill site, but I had to keep trying. I strayed from the standard script and talked to the miners as friends. I knew all their names by now. "I'll buy you a steak myself if you bang on the ceiling down there," I said. "Hold on, they're drilling down to you right now. Everyone in the country is praying for you. Millions of prayers."

I sat down on my equipment case, talking into the probe until I thought my voice would give out. The sun cast fire-tinged shadows on the cows, and the crickets began to chirp. "We're not going to give up on you. You're not alone down there. We're coming to help you," I croaked. Still no answer. Yet it didn't matter. Sitting there alone, talking down into that darkness, I felt something break through inside of me, an absolute sense that God was present. Even if the miners couldn't hear me, God could. And the more I talked, the more hopeful I felt. "You're not alone," I said again. "God is there with you."

At around eight o'clock that night, Jeff called me from the drill site to tell me the first rescue drill had been fixed. My back aching, my voice almost gone, I said into my headset, "Hang on, we're getting closer." It was almost ten o'clock when I drove to the nearby Wal-Mart to park and grab a few hours of sleep in my car. But once more, sleep wouldn't come.

I returned early Saturday morning and started talking into the probe again, sipping a warm cup of the Stanczyks' coffee. I felt better just talking. The words became part of one long prayer, even the standard protocol words. I was off by myself, far from the grating noise of the drill, from the hubbub of rescue workers and reporters, yet I felt completely connected.

I kept at it until around nine P.M., when Jeff called me over to the drill site. Shortly after ten P.M. the drill finally broke through to the mine chamber, 240 feet below the surface. The air compressor was removed from the pilot hole, but it would still be awhile before the rescue capsule was ready. I suggested using my probe in the pilot hole to try to make contact. At last I got the okay.

The machinery was shut off and an eerie quiet fell over the exhausted crowd. I'd been trying to contact the miners for two days, yet now the thought of it struck me cold. *What if there's still no answer at all?* I thought. I put on the headset and knelt over the hole as we began lowering the probe . . . fifty feet, one hundred feet. I started talking again. "Stay where you are. Can you hear me?" There was silence. "Can you hear me?" I asked again, almost begging for a response. *Lord, please let them hear me.*

"Yes . . . we can hear you."

Had I imagined it?

"Can you hear me?" I asked once more, still lowering the probe.

The voice came again, louder and stronger. "We definitely can hear you."

I wanted to shout in jubilation. But first I had to convince myself.

"Are you the trapped miners?" It was more of a statement than a question.

"Yes." Awe swept over me. It was almost as if God himself had spoken to me. I turned to the workers clustered around me and gave them a thumbs-up.

A low murmur of excitement rippled through the crowd.

"How many of you are there?" I asked.

"Nine of us are here."

I held up nine fingers. There was an almost simultaneous sigh of relief, though everyone restrained themselves since the miners' families still had to be notified. Then the miner I was speaking to asked about several people by name. I later learned they were the miners who'd nearly also been trapped. I was touched that after three days underground their first concern was for their fellow workers.

Soon the rescue team swung into action. One by one each weary, coal-covered miner was lifted up in the escape capsule. It was three-thirty A.M. on Sunday when I finally put my equipment back in my trunk and said goodbye to the Stanczyks. I got into my car and headed home to my family.

I had no idea when my cell phone rang three days before that I'd play some small part in a rescue that captivated the entire nation. The miners were safe because God had answered millions of prayers that day. My own problems had been getting the best of me lately. But now I know that when we call on him, we are always answered.

The Miracle of Love

Someday, Maria

EDDIE ALBERT

January 1962

*S*omeday, Maria, someone is going to say a silly thing to you. "Maria," he'll say, and he'll be very solemn, "you must always be grateful to Mr. Albert for choosing you out of all those children."

And the trouble is, Maria, that you just might believe him. Because you are beautiful, because I adore you, because your hair is long and your eyes enormous, because you are seven years old and have me completely wrapped around your little finger . . . you might actually believe that I stepped into that orphanage, looked around at all the children, and selected you. But I didn't, Maria. I wasn't the one who chose you at all.

It was three years ago that I had dinner in Paris with Art Buchwald. It was the first time I'd been away from Margo and young Edward, and I missed them terribly. Only one thing cast a shadow when I thought of my family—there wasn't enough of it! Margo and I never dreamed of having just one child. After

Edward's birth, when no brothers or sisters came, we placed our name with adoption agencies all over the country. Years went by, but no child came to live with us.

That evening in Paris I was sounding off to Art on the slow pace of adoption. He laid down his fork. "We have three adopted kids," he said, "and we didn't wait years and years to get them. We found one in England, one in France, and one in Spain—and you couldn't ask for finer youngsters."

He leaned across the table. "It would break your heart to see some of those orphanages. Why, we saw one in Spain that had over two thousand children."

It was one of those strange moments when everything seems to make sense, even the language. Margo was born in Mexico and speaks Spanish fluently. I went to the telephone and talked to her in California. The next day I was bound for Madrid and that orphanage with its two thousand children.

Once on the plane, the enormity of what I was doing swept over me. How was I going to pick the right child from two thousand?

Psychiatry, I thought. I'd pick a child who looked healthy and bright and then take him or her to a psychiatrist for tests. I lowered the seat back; I was tired.

But sleep wouldn't come. Suddenly I realized that psychiatry could not really define the special magic that makes one person belong with another.

I remembered what I'd learned long ago, that the only valid position for viewing a decision is eternity, that the only One who sees from there is God. I'd asked him to guide me in lesser matters; why not in this one? Did I really have more confidence in myself than in him? The children in the orphanage were his children, just as Margo and Edward and I were. He knew which one belonged with us.

But how would I know? How would I be shown his choice for our family? As soon as I asked the question, I knew the answer. God's choice would be the first child I saw.

There in the plane I bowed my head. "Lord," I said, "I'll take that first child."

This time, I got to sleep.

Early the next morning I was sitting in the office of the director of the great gray-walled orphanage.

"And what kind of child do you have in mind?" he asked in English.

"I would not be so impertinent as to say," I told him.

The director stared at me, then at the paper he'd been writing on. "You have one son, age seven. So I suppose you would like a girl?"

"A girl would be fine."

The director scrutinized me for a moment. Abruptly he picked up the phone and spoke a few words in Spanish. I wondered if he heard my heart pounding as we waited.

The door opened and a nun led in a little girl. I stared at her, gulped, and closed my eyes.

"Lord!" I prayed. "You don't mean it!"

For there in front of me you stood, Maria—the toughest, most defiant, dirtiest four-year-old I had ever seen. You stood with your feet planted wide apart, your eyes on the floor.

I looked from you to the director. He was watching me nervously, apologetically, retaining the nun in order to whisk you away when the American exploded. I suddenly knew that this was not the first time you had been shown to a prospective parent. Suspicions stabbed me. You might be a behavior problem . . .

"How do we go about adopting her?" My words came quickly.

The director stared at me as if he hadn't heard right. Then he sprang from his chair so hastily he almost knocked it over and plunked you into my lap. And so, with your feather weight on my knee, I heard the director outline procedures. The Spanish government required certain papers; the United States required others.

I hardly listened. For, was I imagining it, or was there a gentle pressure against my chest? I leaned forward half an inch; the tiny pressure increased.

My proud Maria, before you responded to me, you were testing me to see if I would respond to you. It was a kind of unspoken proposition with no loss of face: *I could love you if you loved me.* My brave Maria!

I didn't see you again for two whole weeks while the slow, legal part of the adoption got started. My first job was to tell Margo that we had a daughter. I'd call her and talk about mechanics—she would have to deal with the immigration authorities, find a welfare agency to sponsor us . . . Then there was Margo's voice from California, asking the one question I'd been pretending she wouldn't ask.

"Oh, Eddie, describe her to me!"

I suppose that was the longest pause ever run up on a transatlantic phone call. Then I remembered a photograph I'd once seen of Margo as a child; she was all skinny arms and legs.

"Honey," I said, "she reminds me a lot of you."

One day, while we were waiting for final papers, the orphanage gave me permission to take you out for lunch. At the restaurant you scraped your plate clean while I was unfolding my napkin. Then you ate my lunch too.

In the taxi going back, you sat close to me, studying my face. That is why you didn't see the orphanage until we had stopped in front of it. You looked out at the gray walls, then back at me.

Maria! How could I have known? How could I have guessed?

Somehow no one in the orphanage had explained to you that this was only a visit, only a lunch. So many children, the overworked nuns, and no one to read in your eyes that you thought this was the day of adoption, the final leave-taking. And now I had brought you back!

You flung yourself, shrieking, to the sidewalk. And I, with my miserable lack of Spanish, could not explain. I knelt beside you, begging you to believe me. "I'm coming back! Mañana, Maria! Tomorrow!" When a nun came out to get you, we were both sitting in the middle of the sidewalk, crying our eyes out.

I did come back, the next day, and the next, until the unbelievable day when you were ours.

It was twenty-four hours from Madrid to Los Angeles. You sat on my lap the entire plane trip; you would not sleep.

We were a pretty groggy pair when we stumbled off the plane in California and into Margo's arms. She let loose a machine-gun volley of Spanish, the only word of which I understood was, "Mama."

Going home you sat in her lap, and for weeks afterward I was a lucky man if I got so much as a glance.

At home Margo tucked you into bed. And still you would not close your eyes. You'd been without sleep for thirty-six hours, but you didn't want to let Margo out of your sight. At last you pointed to her wedding band.

"Give me your ring," you said.

Margo slipped off the ring and placed it in your hand. "Now you can't leave me," you said. A second later you were asleep.

And Edward, how did he feel about this possible competition for our love? We soon found out. You had lungs that could summon the fire department, but whenever I asked you to speak more quietly, Edward would give me a look of deep reproach.

"Papa! Of course she shouts! There were two thousand kids making a racket; she had to yell to be heard."

Any correction you received had to be while Edward was out of the room. And you felt the same way about him. I'll never forget the day the school bully knocked Edward down and you knocked down the bully. They tell me you were banging his head on the floor when a teacher pulled you off.

I love the toughness in you. I love your loyalty. I love your quick mind. I even love your noise (but not while Papa's napping, all right, honey?).

I think you are the most beautiful little girl in the world, and sometimes, watching you, I think, *How in all the world did I find you?*

Then I remember. I didn't find you. I didn't do it at all.

The Duel

CATHERINE MOORE

February 1985

Watch out! You nearly broadsided that car!" my father yelled at me. "Can't you do anything right?!"

Those words hurt worse than blows. I turned my head toward the elderly man in the seat beside me, daring me to challenge him. A lump rose in my throat as I averted my eyes. I wasn't prepared for another battle.

"I saw the car, Dad. Please don't yell at me when I'm driving." My voice was measured and steady, sounding far calmer than I really felt. Dad glared at me, then turned away and settled back.

At home I left Dad in front of the television and went outside to collect my thoughts. Dark, heavy clouds hung in the air with a promise of rain. The rumble of distant thunder seemed to echo my inner turmoil. What could I do about him?

Dad had been a lumberjack in the great woods of Washington and Oregon. He'd enjoyed being outdoors, and he'd reveled in pitting his strength against the forces of nature. He'd entered the grueling lumberjack competitions so popular in our area, and he had placed very often. The walls of his house were filled with trophies that attested to his prowess.

But the years marched on relentlessly. The first time he couldn't lift a heavy log, he joked about it; but later that same day I saw him outside alone straining to lift it. He became irritable whenever anyone teased him about his advancing age or when he couldn't do something he had done as a younger man.

Four days after his sixty-seventh birthday, he'd had a heart attack. An ambulance sped him to the hospital while a paramedic administered CPR to keep blood and oxygen flowing to his brain. At the hospital Dad was rushed into an operating room. He was lucky; he survived.

But something inside Dad died. His zest for life was gone. He obstinately refused to follow doctor's orders. Suggestions and offers of help were turned aside with sarcasm and insults. The number of visitors thinned, then finally stopped altogether. Dad was left alone.

My husband, Dick, and I asked Dad to come live with us on our small farm. We hoped the fresh air and rustic atmosphere would help Dad adjust. Within a week after he moved in, I regretted the invitation. It seems nothing was satisfactory. He criticized everything I did. I became frustrated and moody. Soon I was taking out my pent-up anger on Dick. We began to bicker and argue. Alarmed, Dick sought out our pastor and explained the situation. The clergyman set up weekly counseling appointments for us. At the close of each session he prayed, asking God to soothe Dad's troubled mind. But the months wore on and God was silent.

A raindrop struck my cheek, I looked up into the dull, gray sky. Somewhere up there was "God." Although I believed a Supreme Being had created the universe, I had difficulty believing the God cared or even knew about the tiny human beings on this earth. And now I was tired of waiting for a God who didn't answer. Something had to be done and it was up to me to do it.

The next day I sat down with the phone book and methodically telephoned each of the mental health clinics listed in the Yellow Pages. I explained my problem to each of the nameless, sympathetic voices that answered—in vain, it seemed. Just when I was giving up hope, one of the voices suddenly exclaimed, "I just read something that might help you! Let me go get the article." Hardly daring to breathe, I listened as she read. The article described a remarkable study done at a nursing home. All of the patients were under treatment for chronic depression. Yet their attitudes, it seemed, had improved dramatically when they were given responsibility for a dog.

I hung up the telephone. *A dog!? Could anything as simple as a pet be the answer?*

I drove to the animal shelter that very afternoon. After I filled out a questionnaire, the uniformed officer led me to the kennels. The odor of disinfectant stung my nostrils as I moved down the row of pens. Each contained five to seven barking, leaping dogs of all descriptions. Longhaired dogs, curly-haired dogs, black dogs, spotted dogs—all jumping up, trying to reach me. I studied each one but mentally rejected one after the other for various reasons: too big, too small, too much hair, whatever. As I neared the last pen, a dog in the shadows of the far corner struggled to his feet, walked to the front of the run and sat down. It was a pointer, one of the dog world's aristocrats. But this was a caricature of the breed. Years had etched his face and muzzle with shades of gray. His hipbones jutted out in lopsided triangles. But it was the eyes that caught and held my attention. Calm and clear, they beheld me unwaveringly.

I pointed to the dog. "Can you tell me about him?" The officer looked, then shook his head in puzzlement.

"He's a funny one. Appeared out of nowhere and sat in front of the gate. We brought him in figuring someone would be right down to claim him. That was two weeks ago, and we've heard nothing. His time is up tomorrow." He gestured helplessly.

As the words sank in I turned to the man in horror. "You mean you're going to kill him?"

"Ma'am," he said gently, "that's our policy. We don't have room for every unclaimed dog."

I looked at the pointer again. The calm brown eyes awaited my decision. "I'll take him," I said impulsively.

I drove home with the dog on the front seat beside me. When I reached the house, I honked twice. I was helping my prize out of the car when Dad shuffled onto the front porch.

"Ta-da! Look what I got for you, Dad!" I said excitedly.

Dad looked, then wrinkled his face in disgust, as though he had seen a particularly nasty species of insect. "If I had wanted a dog I would have gotten one. And I would have picked out a better specimen than that bag of bones. Keep it! I don't want it!" Dad waved his arm scornfully and turned back toward the house.

An anger rose inside me. It squeezed together my throat

muscles, roared up to my head, and pounded into my temples. I followed Dad, dragging the dog with me.

"You had better get used to him, Dad. He's staying!" Dad ignored me. "Did you hear me, old man?" I screamed.

At those words Dad whirled angrily, his hands clenched tightly at his sides, eyes narrowed and ablaze with hate. We stood glaring at each other like duelists, tension creating an unbridgeable chasm between us. Suddenly the pointer pulled free from my grasp. He wobbled toward my dad and sat down in front of him. Then slowly, carefully, he raised his right paw.

Dad's lower jaw trembled as he stared at the uplifted paw. Confusion replaced the anger in his eyes. The pointer waited patiently. Then Dad was on his knees hugging the animal.

It was the beginning of a warm and intimate friendship. Dad named the pointer Cheyenne. Together he and Cheyenne explored the community. They spent long hours walking down dusty lanes. They spent reflective moments on the banks of streams, angling for tasty trout. They even started to attend Sunday services together, Dad sitting quietly in a pew and Cheyenne lying quietly at his feet.

Dad and Cheyenne were inseparable throughout the next three years. Dad's bitterness faded, and he and Cheyenne made many friends. Then late one night I was startled to feel Cheyenne's cold nose burrowing through our bed covers. He had never before come into our bedroom at night! I woke Dick, put on my robe, and ran into my father's room. Dad lay in his bed, his face serene. But his spirit had left quietly sometime during the night. As I stood staring at his peaceful expression,

Dick came, checked my father's pulse, then gently guided me from the room.

Two days later my shock and grief deepened when I discovered Cheyenne lying dead beside Dad's bed. I wrapped his still form in the rag rug he had slept on beside Dad's bed. As Dick and I buried him near a favorite fishing hole, I silently thanked the dog for the help he had given me in restoring Dad's peace of mind.

The morning of Dad's funeral dawned overcast and dreary. *This day looks like the way I feel,* I thought as I walked down the aisle to the pews reserved for family. I was surprised to see the many friends Dad and Cheyenne had made filling the church. The pastor began his eulogy. It was a tribute to both Dad and the dog who had changed his life. And then the pastor turned to Hebrews 13:2. "Be not forgetful to entertain strangers, for thereby some have entertained angels unawares.' I've often thanked God for sending that angel," he said.

For me, the shadows of the past melded together and dropped into place, completing a puzzle that I had not seen before . . . the sympathetic voice that had just read the right article . . . Cheyenne's unexpected appearance at the animal shelter . . . his calm acceptance and complete devotion to my father . . . and the close proximity of their deaths. . . . And suddenly I understood. I knew that God had answered my prayers after all.

His Mysterious Ways

MY HUSBAND, Rich, who'd been adopted as a baby, always brushed aside questions about whether he'd like to find his birth parents, saying, "If they didn't want me then, it's too late now." Still I knew that his stoic surface hid a deep ache. One night I noticed Rich crying at a TV movie about a father and son. I decided to track down his birth family so he might find some closure.

All I had to go on was the information on Rich's birth certificate: his birthdate, October 16, 1941; his mother's name, Ruth Hicks Casselman; and her place of birth, Waupaca County, Wisconsin. I wrote to the hospital, went through old phone directories, and searched the Internet—but no luck.

The only place left to try was the National Archives in Washington, D.C. One day in November 1999, I went to check the census records there. But I learned that by law, census information isn't released for seventy-two years. I was crushed. What good was such dated material?

I pulled the latest Waupaca census reel available—1920—from its file drawer. As I passed the first rows of microfilm readers, I overheard a man mention Wisconsin to the older woman with him. *That's interesting,* I thought before going on to my reader.

There was a listing for Hicks—Ruth! Encouraged, I went back for the 1910 reel. Maybe I could get names of relatives to follow up on. The slot where the reel should have been was empty. Then I remembered the folks I had overheard.

I walked over and peeked at their screen. Ruth Hicks, Waupaca County, 1910! Amazed, I asked, "May I take a look when you're done? I'm trying to locate the family of Ruth Hicks . . ."

". . . Casselman?" the woman gasped. "She was my mother! Our family split up when I was little and I'm trying to find my baby brother. I've been looking for him for years."

Later that evening over dinner, the last chapter in the family history was finally closed. Shirley Casselman Garnett met her long-lost baby brother, my husband, Rich.

—JAN NOBLE, *January 2001*

A New Pair of Shoes

WILLIE B. RABORN

April 1986

Keeping up had seemed so important when I was a teenager. Back in 1963, I can remember that if you weren't wearing penny loafers, you'd just as soon go around in your bare feet. I was thirteen years old and had worked hard to keep up with my peers. I had only one serious problem that year. I had bought oxfords—but penny loafers were "in." I asked my dad for help.

"I need some money for penny loafers," I told him one afternoon at the shop where he worked as a car mechanic.

"Willie," he said in apparent shock, "the shoes you have on aren't a month old yet! Why do you need new ones?"

"Everybody's wearing penny loafers, Dad."

"That might be, Son, but that doesn't make it any easier for me to pay for them." Dad's salary was small and seldom covered more than rent and groceries.

"Dad, I look like a fool wearing these things." I pointed to the nearly new oxfords I had on.

Dad looked at me for a full minute before he answered. "Tell you what I'll do," he said. "Wear those shoes one more day. Look at every pair of shoes you see at school. If you can come here after school and tell me that you are worse off than the other kids, I'll take part of your mom's grocery money for you to buy some new shoes."

Triumphantly, I went to school the next morning, knowing that it would be the last day I'd have to appear out of style. I did what Dad said, but I had no intention of telling him the results.

Brown shoes, black ones, stained white tennis shoes—they all seemed to have a personality of their own. By noon I'd seen shoes that were scuffed beyond recognition, torn shoes like none I'd ever had to wear, and shoes with holes in them that made me wonder how the kids wearing them ever kept their feet dry on rainy days. And then there were those gleaming black penny loafers with the horseshoe taps that demanded attention when they clicked in the halls.

When school was out, I rushed to the shop where Dad worked, knowing I'd return to school the following Monday as a part of the "in" crowd. Every now and then, I dragged my heels on the pavement, imagining how the taps would sound when they were in place later that night.

The shop was quiet when I arrived. Only an occasional clank of metal could be heard as Dad worked under a 1956 Chevy. Even the smell of old motor oil pleased me that day. One man sat alone in the shop waiting for Dad to finish with the transmission of his car.

"Mr. Alva," I said to the man waiting to get his car, "is Dad almost finished?"

"Can't ever tell, Will. You know your dad. He's working on the linkage on the transmission, but if he sees anything else wrong, he'll fix that too."

I walked to the car to wait. All I could see were Dad's legs from the knees down. I stood there absent-mindedly fingering the taillight of the Chevy as I stared unconsciously at Dad's feet and legs.

His blue work pants were oil-stained and faded. His shoes were old and black, the kind mechanics and service station attendants wear. The left one had two stitches of baling wire where the soles had long since separated. The laces had been spliced on both shoes. Neither one had a heel, only small, bent nails where the heel had been pulled off. Dad had bent them to keep them from pushing through to his feet.

"That you back there, boy?" Dad said, coming out from under the car.

"Yes, sir," I said.

"You do what I told you today?"

"Yes, sir."

"Well, what do you want to do?" He looked as though he might know what my answer would be.

"I still want the penny loafers." I forced myself not to look at his shoes.

"I have to take your mom grocery shopping as soon as I get off work. Why don't you go ahead now and get the shoes."

Dad handed me ten dollars and fished in his pocket for a quarter to pay the three percent sales tax. I took the money and went to the store two blocks down the street.

I stopped in front of the store window to see if the shoes were still on sale. They were, for $9.95, but I wouldn't have enough money left to buy the necessary taps. I decided to wait until we got home and ask Mom for the money. I couldn't ask Dad for more right then.

When I thought of Dad, his old shoes flashed through my mind. I could see the mended soles, the spliced laces, the bent nails in the heels. He had worn the leather off his shoes working for us, his family. Surely his feet got cold on those nights when he got calls to go across town to start someone's car, yet he never complained. I thought of clients like Mr. Alva, whom Dad was always doing something extra for, even if they never asked. I thought of Dad going without things he needed, so I could have things I wanted. Soon the gleam on the loafers in the window started to dull.

What if Dad had been like me? What kind of shoes would I be wearing?

I went inside. I saw a rack on a far wall that appeared to hold a million pairs of black penny loafers. On a rack next to it was a sign that said, "Clearance 50% Off." Below the sign sat several "young" versions of Dad's shoes.

My mind was playing Ping-Pong. First I'd think of Dad's old shoes and then the new ones. I'd imagine keeping up with the "in" crowd at school. And then I'd picture Dad—tireless, selfless, almost Christ-like in the sacrifices he was willing to make for his family. When it came to "keeping up," which ideal was worth following?

I took a size ten from the clearance rack and darted to the checkout counter. Tax included, the shoes came to $6.13.

I ran back to the shop and put Dad's new shoes in his car. I went into the shop and gave him the change I had left.

"I thought the shoes were $9.95," he said.

"They were on sale." I took a broom from the nearby wall and started helping Dad sweep up. At five o'clock he signaled that it was time to go.

Dad picked up the box when we got in the car. When he opened it, he just stared without saying a word. He looked first at the shoes and then at me.

"I thought you were going to get those penny loafers," he said.

"I was, Dad, but—" I couldn't explain the rest. How could I tell Dad that his was the image I had chosen to follow? Or that when it came to "keeping up," I wanted to try to keep up with the very best? I wanted to be more like the good man God had given me for a father.

Dad put his hand on my shoulder and we sat looking at each other for a moment. Nothing else was said. Dad started the car and we went home.

Strong Enough to Cry

Marion Bond West

February 2002

*E*lberton, Georgia, my hometown, was only an hour's drive for my husband, Gene, and me, but today it felt like light years. My mother had died three weeks earlier. Gene and I had to take care of some final affairs at the bank where she'd worked for thirty-eight years. As we drew near to Elberton, I felt an oppressive, almost physical sense of sadness creep over me. But I fought it off.

We drove into town and circled the neatly manicured town square that was filled with marigolds and zinnias blooming lusciously in the summer heat. Gene reached over and took my hand, but I stared straight ahead like a store mannequin. He glanced at me. "Honey, is it too soon to do this?" he asked.

"Of course not," I said. "I can handle it." After all, my mother had lived a long and happy life. She was ninety-two, had been in good health for most of her life, and had devoted family and friends. My rational mind told me how fortunate she and I both had been, that death was a natural part of life. And so, being reasonable, I hadn't cried at all—not through her long illness and her eventual hospitalization, not even at her funeral or at the cemetery. It didn't make sense for me to break down. Mother would have wanted me to hold up.

"Ready to go to the bank?" Gene asked.

"Well, sure, that's what we came for."

We were headed for the new, fancy bank building where my mother had been assistant vice president until she retired back in 1974. The original brick and granite bank still stood solidly on the north corner of the square. Now it was the headquarters of the town newspaper. That was the building I remembered from my childhood, the place where my mother worked. My father had died suddenly of strep throat in 1938 just before penicillin came into widespread use, so Mother became our sole support. She was twenty-nine at the time, and I was almost two.

When she first started, the bank had all of three employees—a president, vice president, and Mother, who did everything from sweeping the floor to shining the spittoons. Back then, I didn't think much about how Mother had to walk a mile and a half to work every day, then back again, through the broiling summers and windy winters. Naturally I assumed that all mothers economized by digging into their lipsticks with a bobby pin to get the last bit of color.

She was tall, slim, and beautiful. I loved being seen with her. She wore her thick, dark hair pulled back, which accentuated her Clara Bow mouth and set off her dimples. She wore elegant second-hand tailored clothes, sent to her by my aunt in New York who did part-time modeling, and White Shoulders perfume, just a dab so a bottle would last forever. Until I was old enough to go to school, when Mother was at work I stayed with a next-door neighbor. When I felt the urge, I would lift the receiver off the tall black phone so I could tell the operator, "Number seven, please."

"Granite City Bank, Jewette Bond speaking," my mother would answer. Those words thrilled me every time. "Hey, Mother," I'd say. "Mannie!" she'd exclaim. "How's my girl?"

Now, as Gene and I drove past the old bank building, I stared at the small ground-floor window that had looked into her office. On the way to the drugstore for a cherry Coke after school, my friends and I would peek into the tiny window, and scratch on the screen. My mother would look up from the keys of her Royal typewriter, hop up from her swivel chair, and open the heavy glass front door to give me a hug. "How was your day, Mannie?"

Mother had Wednesday afternoons off, and it was my favorite time of the week. Most of all I remembered the swelter-ing summers, when there wasn't a breeze to stir our kitchen cur-tains. Mother and I would thump on the watermelons being sold from the back of a farmer's old truck until we found the perfect one. At home, Mother would wear light blue shorts and go bare-foot, just like me. She would put a piece of newspaper on our kitchen table, heave the melon on top, then cut into it. There was a satisfying splitting sound, and I would stand on tiptoe to get the first glimpse of the rosy insides. We had picked a good one all right! We would take the thick slices and sit on our back steps, sinking our faces into the juicy melon, laughing and spitting out seeds while the juice ran down our arms.

I could almost taste that long-ago sweetness as Gene and I

drove through Elberton to the sleek new Granite City Bank—now called Regions Bank—that was located a block farther down from the main square. As long as I could remember, Mother had had a safe-deposit box in the bank, and it was one of the things she'd mentioned in the months before she died. "Remember the lockbox, Mannie," she'd said. "I know, Mother," I'd say, rubbing lotion into her frail hands—hands that had once been so strong, that had held me when I hurt, that typed for hours at the bank, that were always folded in prayer at the end of the day.

We parked, then Gene and I walked into the building. The air conditioning gave out an almost arctic chill, but we were greeted warmly by the employees, many of whom had known my mother. I took a deep breath and forced myself to smile. *It would be so embarrassing to cry in front of them,* I thought.

One of the cashiers showed us into the area where lockboxes covered the walls. She handed me a big manila envelope. "You can put everything in this," she said. Gene helped me open the box. I emptied its entire contents into the big envelope—a jumble of bank books, wrinkled papers, old coins, and a box rattling with jewelry. I felt my throat tightening. "Don't you want to look at what's there?" Gene asked. "Later," I said.

When we got back in the car, I sagged with relief. Thank goodness I hadn't broken down or gotten emotional. Gene started driving. I reached into the envelope and pulled out a letter on onionskin paper, yellowed with age, that I recognized as being typed on Mother's old Royal. I unfolded the pages and looked at the date on the top. June 27, 1938. Just after my father died.

"My Precious Baby," it began. I held my breath as I read

down the page. "Mannie, you were a baby wanted very badly by both your daddy and mother." As far as my mother was concerned "a better soul never lived" than my daddy. She went on to tell how happy they had been together because they understood each other perfectly.

I read on, blinking rapidly. "Mother wishes for you a very happy life. I hope and pray a lot of good things will come your way. May God watch over you and keep you always. To me, your being here is the dearest thing on earth. With all my love, Mother."

I held the yellowed pages in my hand, overcome by emotion. This was a letter that my mother had meant for me to read after she was gone.

"You hungry?" Gene asked. Without waiting for an answer, he pulled into the parking lot of a fast-food restaurant. Parked alongside the lot entrance was an old beat-up truck, its bed piled high with watermelons, just like the trucks from my childhood. "Gene! Watermelons! Let's get a big one!"

Gene was concentrating on lunch. "Not now, honey," he said. "It might split and make a mess." He hopped out of the car and headed toward the restaurant. For a moment I sat there stunned. Maybe I'd just sit in the awful heat and slowly melt like a stick of butter. *Lord, what is the matter with me?*

"Marion?" It was Gene calling from the restaurant doorway, looking puzzled. *Breathe,* I told myself. *Move.* I stuffed the letter into the envelope, got out of the car as if in a trance, and went in and sat at a table. Gene was ready to get in line and order. "What do you want, honey?"

"Nothing," I murmured. Gene came back with his hamburger

and fries. I sat desperately trying to reason with my emotions. *Oh, Lord, what grown woman falls apart in the middle of McDonald's? Help me keep it together!* I tilted my head back to keep the tears in my eyes, fighting to regain composure. I lost the battle. As people around us kindly looked away, I crumpled. I buried my face in my hands and began to cry, hard, from a place deep inside, a place where my love for Mother was rooted. She must have experienced a similar wrenching grief when Daddy died. She had been so strong for me. Yet my Aunt Liz had told me how Mother had cried after Daddy's funeral.

It seemed like an eternity until I uncovered my face. Gene held out his handkerchief. "It's okay, Marion," he said. "Can I get you anything?"

"Yes," I said and told him.

In an instant Gene was up and out the door. I watched from the window as he handed some money to the man at the watermelon truck, then opened our trunk so he could lift it in.

"Put it up front with me!" I cried, bolting from the table and running outside to get in the car.

I slipped off my sandals and propped my bare feet on the watermelon's cool skin. I knew the pain and grief I'd felt pressing on my heart would never go away altogether. Why should they? The more you love, the more loss hurts. But as we drove past the old bank building for the last time, new feelings stirred inside me—peace, acceptance, understanding. Mother was gone, but God would help me endure. Still, I could cry when I needed a good thorough cleansing. Yes, love makes loss hard. But it also makes us strong—strong enough to cry.

Uncle Ornery

BRENDA KNUTSON

July 2002

I rounded the bend in the road on the way to the VA home where Uncle Orville lived. It was Memorial Day, and my kids, my husband, and I were making the hour-long drive to the home's family picnic. The kids had never met Uncle Orville. I'd hardly seen him myself in the last thirty years, and I wasn't particularly looking forward to it today. *It's your duty to check on him,* I reminded myself once more. *He's family.*

Uncle Orville had lived in a room in my family's house when I was young. The day before Orville arrived, Dad sat us all down and told us a little about his brother. Uncle Orville had been a high school basketball star, good-looking and popular. He joined the army in 1943 at age eighteen and was shipped out to Europe, where he saw immediate action at the ferocious Battle of the Bulge. He returned with scars deeper than anybody could see, my father said. And that's when Uncle Orville started drinking. By the time he came to live with us, he'd been an alcoholic for decades.

He'd even spent time in jail for drunk driving. Except for meals, he stayed shut up in his room, not even joining us for church.

Uncle Orville had his good days, though. He'd suddenly volunteer to do some plumbing or yard work. He loved Mom's cooking and liked to tell her so. Once he bought me a brand-new pair of warm woolen mittens. I looked up at his blue-gray eyes, and for a moment they seemed to shine. But those moments were few and far between, and I never felt a real connection to Uncle Orville.

By the time he was sixty, drinking and hard manual labor had taken their toll. Uncle Orville moved into a VA home. After Dad died, Mom continued to visit him there every month. I was married by then and living nearby, so I accompanied her on a few of those trips. She would bring him a chocolate malt from Dairy Queen, which he'd suck down, hardly even looking at us.

Shortly after Mom died in 1992, I was sifting through her papers and found an invitation to the Memorial Day family picnic at the veterans' home. I was about to toss it, but Uncle Orville was family. It would be wrong of me not to look in on him as my parents had. I thought about those moments when I would see something light up in his eyes, a spark of the person he was before he went to war. But I also remembered all those uncomfortable times when he would not speak and would not even look at me. I often wondered if he wanted anyone to get close to him.

Uncle Orville refused to come down and join us at the Memorial Day picnic. We offered to go up to his room, but a nurse told us he wouldn't have it. Finally the nurse led him onto a balcony so we could wave to him and show him the table we'd decorated with balloons and American flags. He nodded to us, unsmiling, before scuttling back inside.

Well, we tried, I thought. Uncle Orville clearly didn't want companionship. I was actually relieved; he just seemed like too much work. *Uncle Ornery is more like it,* I thought to myself. But a week later I received an envelope full of paperwork that I needed to sign to become Uncle Orville's legal representative in place of Mom. I would have to go back to the VA home. But that didn't mean I had to visit Uncle Orville.

I dropped off the papers and started to leave when my conscience pricked at me. *All right, I'll just say hello.* I found him lying in bed, staring into space. "Who are you?" he demanded.

"Brenda," I said, "Keith's daughter. You remember. You used to live with us." I talked some more and showed him some pictures of my boys. Uncle Orville didn't seem to give a hoot.

"Nice of you to stop by," he said brusquely. "But you don't have to visit me. In fact, don't . . . don't come at all."

That would have been all right with me. I'd tried my best. But I discovered I had to return every twelve weeks to meet with Uncle Orville's caseworker. *Fine,* I thought. *I'll schedule my appointments at times when Orville would be at lunch.*

Despite my businesslike approach, I learned new things about Uncle Orville. "On Trivial Pursuit days," his caseworker said, "Orville sits off in the corner away from the group, but every so often we'll hear the correct answers coming from him." I also learned how he kept trying to get out of the home. One evening after dinner, he just wandered off without anyone noticing. When he came back, the doors were locked. Orville ended up spending the night under a bridge. And I found myself sticking up for him.

"Why don't you invite him to play Trivial Pursuit? Why don't you keep better track of him?" I asked.

Once again I tried to break through to Uncle Orville. *Lord,* I prayed before my next attempt, *I know you love him. Show me how.* I was inspired by Mom's old tactic, and Uncle Orville's eyes lit up the moment I stepped through the door with a Dairy Queen malt. He sucked it down slowly, and I talked about my family. Once the straw went dry, he bolted up and gruffly directed me to the door.

I decided that I could be just as stubborn as he was. I started visiting Uncle Orville between appointments, each time with a chocolate malt in hand. The more silent and sullen he was, the more I talked. I'd update him on the family.

One day he just said, "I got frostbite at the Battle of the Bulge." He told me what had happened and how it felt. Now each time I visited, he told a story, many of them about growing up with my father. His blue-gray eyes and the way he shrugged his shoulders began to remind me of Dad. Still, after twenty minutes or so together, he'd abruptly stand up and show me the door.

Uncle Orville came down with pneumonia and ended up in the hospital. His fever skyrocketed, and he was in a lot of pain, barely able to breathe even with oxygen. While I sat with him, the army chaplain came into the room. "Can I do anything?" he asked.

"Could you read the Twenty-third Psalm?" I asked, although I didn't know if Uncle Orville even knew the Bible.

The chaplain started, "The Lord is my shepherd . . ."

"Okay, okay," Uncle Orville interrupted. "You don't have to

continue. You can go now." Then with a wave of his hand, he sent the chaplain out the door.

Uncle Orville's eyes fixed on mine. "Are you certain there's a God? Even with the wars and all the other ugliness happening in the world?"

"Of course I am," I said. While I drove home later, it struck me how lonely Uncle Orville must be. He didn't even have God in his life. *No wonder . . .*

One night, I got a call from the hospital. "Your uncle is very agitated, and none of us can calm him down."

"Be careful, he's throwing a fit," said the nurse as she fled from Uncle Orville's room when I arrived.

Uncle Orville was sitting bolt upright in bed, a frantic look in his eyes. "What's wrong, Uncle Orville?"

He looked right at me. "How would you like it if you knew you were going straight to hell?" he demanded

I was stunned. "Is that really what you think?" I asked. I saw the fear and sadness in his eyes. I thought of all the pain he'd had in his life. War. Alcoholism. Jail. Dementia.

Briefly he'd been a local sports hero. Then came the war and those scars Dad said no one could see. Yet I could see those scars now as I stood in his hospital room and looked at the man sitting scared in his bed. Thin, tired and reaching out for something—anything—to believe in, even hell.

"Uncle Orville, you're not alone," I said. "You have me. And you have God. You are his child and he loves you unconditionally. You can always be sure of that. Always."

For once, Uncle Orville actually asked me to stay. I held his hand. He didn't pull it back. The next step was hard. I didn't want him to push me away. I prayed. Silently at first, then out loud. Uncle Orville's hand tightened on mine.

I visited Uncle Orville more frequently in the next few weeks as he got sicker and sicker. He asked me to recite the Twenty-third Psalm to him every time. And during each visit, Uncle Orville told me more about his life—how he and Dad would run to school backward in the winter to avoid getting hit face-first by the harsh prairie winds or how he'd hide behind the piano to hear his sister's lessons.

Now I was the one who had to end the visit and leave each time. He'd always ask, "When are you coming back?" It got to the point where I waited for him to fall asleep before I'd leave.

One afternoon I found Uncle Orville attached to a respirator, unable to talk. Overwhelmed by all the machines, I chattered on about baseball scores, family, and church breakfasts.

Suddenly, he reached up his hand and touched my cheek. My tears trickled down over his gnarled fingers. He turned his head a little and wrinkled his brow. I could almost hear him say, "Now don't get all mushy on me."

Several nights later, he sat propped up on pillows, huffing and puffing with his eyes closed, off the respirator. "How are those boys of yours?" he asked.

"Great," I said. "How are those lungs of yours?"

"It's been a tough day," he said slowly. "The toughest."

"I can stay as long as you'd like."

"Can you say that psalm for me?" he asked. I helped him take a drink, sat on the edge of his bed, and began, "The Lord is my shepherd . . ."

When I finished, he said, "Again."

I started over, holding his hand. He closed his eyes, as if to concentrate on taking his next breath. I continued, ". . . though I walk through the valley of the shadow . . ." He took one slow breath. His face relaxed. Even as I went on, ". . . and I will dwell in the house of the Lord forever . . ." I knew he was gone.

I don't know how long I sat there. I held his hand for a long time thinking about how quickly I'd come to know and even love this man who had been such a stranger for so many years. How reluctant I'd been at first to reach out when he wouldn't reach back. How wrong I'd been. But mostly I thought about him and about who he was: my father's brother, a high school sports star, a wounded soldier, a drifter, a drunk, a curmudgeon, a storyteller. And in the end, he was what we all are—a child of God.

The Gift of Kindness

The Secret of the Frying Pan

Nanette Bailey

August 1961

I lay propped up on the sofa, pain keeping me from enjoying the autumn color outside my window. The house was cold, and I had asked the new practical nurse—one of a long series of nurses—to build a fire. Mrs. Harmon was silent as she brought in the logs, holding each one at arm's length from her stiff white uniform. Without a word she held a match to the fire and disappeared into the kitchen with my untouched lunch tray.

Mrs. Harmon's silence matched my mood. There was a kind of honesty in silence, an honesty, I reflected bitterly, that you seldom see any more. I was a real estate agent. Not a very successful one, but I had learned to promote, hustle, and maneuver. The world, I had long ago concluded, was run by the dishonest, and the rest of us had to defend ourselves. Each year I strengthened my own defenses, adding a little more cynicism and indifference to my personality.

Sometimes I was a little horrified at the hard, worldly-wise face that looked back at me from the mirror, but I saw little prospect that it would change. And now, to top things off, this crippling arthritis attack! For weeks I hadn't been out of the house, hadn't been free of pain. I could see no point to it: the lost sales, the enforced idleness, the suffering.

Then Mrs. Harmon brought in the frying pan.

In the hours that followed, I watched a little drama that cast a sudden new light on my illness—that lit my whole life with hope. For that fall afternoon, I glimpsed one of the uses God can make of suffering.

Mrs. Harmon gingerly held the frying pan far away from her, as she had the logs. *Here comes a complaint,* I thought. And to make it worse, a complaint was justified. The pan really was an ugly old thing, made of heavy cast iron and thick with the baked-on crust of many years. I should have thrown it out long ago, but it had been Mother's. It reminded me of simpler, happier days. And I really had tried to get it clean. I'd scoured and scrubbed and scraped. Hardly a day had gone by that I didn't worry away at it, but without making a dent in that stubborn crust.

And now, I thought, *I'm going to get a lecture on kitchen hygiene.* Mrs. Harmon, however, said not a word. She carried the offending frying pan to the fire and, as I stared, stopped and laid it across the logs. Only at the door to the kitchen did she speak. "Ever watch fire clean a pan?" she asked.

The rest of the short October afternoon I watched, hypnotized, as the fire went to work. First the old pan sputtered and smoked, as if complaining at this ill-treatment. But after a while it grew silent. A faint glow, red first, then almost white, spread through its body.

As I watched, transfixed, there was a tiny "ping." A piece of the ancient crust had popped off and dropped into the fire. In a few minutes, another piece came loose, and then another. All afternoon the cleansing process went on until finally, as the fire died, the pan turned from white to dull red and then to black again. It was a glowing, lustrous black, like a new pan. No, more beautiful than that. Like an old pan shined in fire.

As the room grew dusky, Mrs. Harmon came in armed with a great stack of hot pads. She reached into the fireplace and lifted the gleaming pan from the coals. For a moment she inspected it in silence. When she spoke, it was in a low voice.

"People go through fire too," she said thoughtfully. "A nurse sees it all the time." She looked down at the pan. "I've seen men and women come out of it as shiny and clean as this pan."

Barefoot to America

LEGSON KAYIRA

April 1964

My mother did not know where America was. I said to her, "Mother, I want to go to America to go to college. Will you give me your permission?"

"Very well," she said. "You may go. When will you leave?"

I did not want to give her time to discover from others in our village how far away America was, for fear that she would change her mind. "Tomorrow," I said.

"Very well," she said. "I will prepare some maize for you to eat along the way."

The next day, October 14, 1958, I left my home in the village of Mpale, in northern Nyasaland, East Africa. I had only the clothes I wore, a khaki shirt and shorts. I carried the two treasures I owned: a Bible and a copy of *The Pilgrim's Progress*. I carried, too, the maize my mother had given me, wrapped in banana leaves, and a small ax for protection.

My goal was a continent and an ocean away, but I did not

doubt that I would reach it.

I have no idea how old I was. Such things mean little in a land where time is always the same. I suppose I was sixteen or eighteen.

My father died when I was very young. In 1952, my mother listened to the words of the missionaries of the Church of Scotland (Presbyterian), and our family became Christian. From the missionaries, I learned to love God. I also learned that if I was ever to be of value to my village, my people, or my country, it would be necessary for me to have an education.

Wenya, which was eight miles away, had a mission primary school. One day when I felt I was ready to study, I walked there.

I learned many things. I learned I was not, as most Africans believed, the victim of my circumstances but the master of them. I learned that as a Christian, I had an obligation to use the talents God had given me to make life better for others.

Later, in high school, I learned about America. I read the life of Abraham Lincoln and grew to love this man who suffered so much to help the enslaved Africans in his country. I read, too, the autobiography of Booker T. Washington, a man born into slavery in America who had risen in dignity and honor to become a bene-factor of his people and his country.

I gradually realized that only in America would I receive the training and opportunities needed to prepare myself to emulate these men in my own land—to become, like them, a leader, or perhaps even the president of my country.

My intention was to make my way to Cairo, where I hoped to get passage on a ship to America. Cairo was over three thousand miles away, a distance I could not comprehend, and I foolishly thought I could walk it in four or five days. In four or five days, I was only about twenty-five miles from home, my food was gone, and I had no money. I did not know what to do, except I knew that I must keep going.

I developed a pattern of travel that became my life for more than a year. Villages were usually five or six miles apart, on forest paths. I would arrive at one in the afternoon and ask if I could work to earn food, water, and a place to sleep. When this was possible, I would spend the night there, then move on to the next village in the morning.

It was not always possible. Tribal languages change every few miles in Africa; often I was among people with whom I could not communicate. This clearly made me a stranger to them, perhaps an enemy; some would not let me into their villages, and I had to sleep in the forests, eating herbs or wild fruit.

I soon discovered that my ax sometimes gave people the impression I had come to fight or to steal, so I bartered the ax for a knife I could carry unseen. I was actually defenseless against the forest animals I dreaded; but although I heard them at night, none of them approached me. Malaria mosquitoes, however, were my constant companions, and I often was sick.

Two comforts sustained me: my Bible and my *Pilgrim's Progress*. Over and over I read my Bible, particularly finding confidence in the promise "Trust in the Lord with all thine heart; and lean not unto thine own understanding. . . . Then shalt thou walk in thy way safely, and thy foot shall not stumble" (Proverbs 3:5, 23).

By the end of 1959, I had walked one thousand miles to

Uganda, where a family took me in, and I found a job making bricks for government buildings. I remained there for six months, and I sent most of my earnings to my mother.

In *Pilgrim's Progress*, I read many times of the tribulations of the Christian who wandered through the wilderness seeking God, and I compared this to my own wanderings toward the goal I believed God had put into my heart. I could not give up, any more than the Christian had given up.

One afternoon at the USIS library in Kampala, I unexpectedly came upon a directory of American colleges. Opening it at random, I saw the name of Skagit Valley College, Mount Vernon, Washington. I had heard that American colleges sometimes gave scholarships to deserving Africans, so I wrote to Dean George Hodson and applied for one. I realized that I might be refused, but I was not discouraged: I would write to one school after another in the directory until I found one that would help me.

Three weeks later, Dean Hodson replied: I was granted a scholarship, and the school would help me find a job. Overjoyed, I went to the American authorities, only to be told that this was not enough. I would need a passport and the roundtrip fare in order to obtain a visa.

I wrote to the Nyasaland government for a passport, but my request was refused because I could not tell them when I was born. I then wrote to the missionaries who had taught me in my childhood, and it was through their efforts that I was granted a passport. But I still could not get the visa at Kampala because I did not have the fare.

Still determined, I left Kampala and resumed my trip northward. So strong was my faith that I used my last money to buy my first pair of shoes: I knew I could not walk into Skagit Valley College in my bare feet. I carried the shoes to save wear and tear on them.

Across Uganda and into the Sudan, the villages were farther apart and the people were less friendly to me. Sometimes I had to walk twenty or thirty miles in a day to find a place to sleep, or to work to earn some food. At last I reached Khartoum, where I learned that there was an American consulate, and I went there to try my luck.

Once again I heard about the entrance requirements, this time from Vice Consul Emmett M. Coxson, but Mr. Coxson wrote to the college about my plight. They sent back a cable. The students, upon hearing about me and my problems, had raised the fare of $1,700 through benefit parties.

I was thrilled and deeply grateful; I was overjoyed that I had judged Americans correctly for their friendship and brotherhood. I was also thankful to God for his guidance, and I pledged my future to his service.

News that I had walked for over two years and twenty-five hundred miles circulated in Khartoum. The Communists came to me and offered to send me to school in Yugoslavia, all expenses paid, including travel, and a subsistence during my studies.

"I am a Christian," I told them, "and I could not be educated into the kind of man I want to be in your godless schools."

They warned me that, as an African, I would have racial difficulties in the United States, but I had read enough in American newspapers to feel this was a diminishing factor. My religion had taught me that men are not perfect, but as long as they strive to be, they will be pleasing to God. The American effort, I felt, was why the land was so blessed.

In December, 1960, carrying my two books and wearing my first suit, I arrived at Skagit Valley College.

In my speech of gratitude to the student body, I disclosed my desire to become prime minister or president of my country, and I noticed some smiles. I wondered if I had said something naive. I do not think so.

When God has put an impossible dream in your heart, he means to help you fulfill it. I believed this to be true when, as an African bush boy, I felt compelled to become an American college graduate. This is to become true in June, when I will graduate from the University of Washington. And if God has given me the dream of becoming president of Nyasaland, this too will become true.

It is when we resist God that we remain nothing. When we submit to him, whatever the sacrifice or hardship, we can become far more than we dare dream.

The Peace We Found in Forgiveness

Jay Meck

October 1975

As I finished the milking that Friday afternoon last October, I was glad I was done early, for now I would have time to do some other chores before supper, and we'd be able to make the pet parade at the New Holland Fair.

I knew how the boys yearned to see that parade, especially our youngest, little Nelson, seven, who'd be home from school any minute. I poked my head out of the barn door. No sign of Nelson yet, but I did see my wife, Ruth, coming out of the basement. She had been storing sweet potatoes for winter. Now she would be preparing an afternoon snack for Nelson, most likely some of that gingerbread he liked so much.

Putting away the milking pails, I thought how nice it was that as a farmer I could be at home during the day to enjoy my family. I loved it when Nelson bounded up our farm lane from school. He'd come back into the barn to tell me what happened that day, his freckled face beaming. Then he'd scurry over to the house to get a nibble from Ruth and dash back down the lane to wait for his older brother Johnny to come home from school. When Johnny appeared, Nelson never failed to say, "Ha-ha, I got home before you. What took you so long?" Then the two of them would race back up to the house.

The routine was always the same and never failed to give me pleasure. How blessed I was, with a wonderful wife and three boys to share the farm.

As I finished putting up the pails, I heard someone running up the lane. Expecting Nelson, I came out of the barn only to be faced with his school-bus driver, Mike.

"Nelson's been hit by a car!" Mike yelled frantically. "Call an ambulance!"

My head suddenly felt light. Ruth yelled from the kitchen door that she would call one.

I tore off wildly down the lane to the road. My heart was racing like a tractor in the wrong gear. My mind was in a tailspin. *Please, Lord, not Nelson!* I thought. *Who could have done this? Who?*

When I reached the road, I pushed my way through the crowd already gathered near the school bus. There on the blacktop of Highway 340 lay my son. I bent down and touched him softly. He didn't move. As I brushed back a fold in his hair, tears stung my eyes.

Just down the highway a car was pulled over and I saw the license plate—the orange and blue colors of New York.

The area where we live—the Dutch country of south-eastern Pennsylvania—attracts a goodly number of tourists, and some of them don't have a very good reputation among us natives.

I stood up over Nelson and in a choking voice asked, "Who hit him?"

There was silence until finally a young dark-haired man and a woman who looked to be his wife stepped forward. They seemed frightened and dazed.

"He just ran out in front of us," the woman said, clutching tightly to the man's arm.

I walked over to them. I'm not a man of violence—in fact I've never so much as laid a finger on anyone, yet my arms felt heavy and my hands tingled. I took a deep breath, unsure of what I should do. "Jay Meck's my name," I said finally.

The man flinched but shook hands with me. Just then the ambulance pulled up and its driver urged Ruth and me to follow. As we drove away, I looked back to see the couple holding on to each other, staring after us.

On our way to Lancaster Hospital, we passed an Amish family, riding in tranquility in a horse and buggy. The New Yorkers, I thought, had intruded upon that kind of peacefulness. They had come here where they didn't belong.

At the emergency room, Dr. Show, the man who had delivered all our boys, met us immediately and said what I'd suspected all along. "Nelson's gone."

The next hours, even days, became a blur. We were besieged with cards and letters. Scores of friends and neighbors dropped by to help with the milking. They brought pies and casseroles. But even surrounded by all the sympathy, Ruth and I found we just couldn't keep little Nelson from our thoughts. He meant too much to us.

Nelson had come into our lives late, almost as if he were a special gift from God. As the youngest, I suppose we held him precious and delighted in him more. But, oh, how much there was to delight in! The Sunday-school librarian called him "Sunshine" because he always had a cheerful disposition and a smile that never seemed to go away. What was most extraordinary about our son was his understanding of Christianity. He had an uncanny sense of caring for others.

In school, for instance, he was the little guy who made friends with all the unfortunates—the physically challenged, the shy children, the outcasts. In the evenings when I'd go to his room to tuck him in, Nelson would be lying in bed with his hands folded. "Boy, Pop," he'd say, "there are sure a lot of people I've got to pray for tonight."

Like other small children, Nelson would squirm in church, but he would then startle Ruth and me by marching out after services and announcing, "I have Jesus in my heart." Other times, he'd come in with a sick bird he'd found and wanted to help, or he'd bring a stranger to our home, some poor soul seeking farm work.

Though older, Bob, eighteen, and Johnny, fifteen, were extremely close to their brother. The following Tuesday, when the funeral was over and we were sitting in our kitchen, Johnny recalled Nelson's daily vigil at the lane after school. "I'll bet

Nelson's up in heaven right now, and when I get there he'll say, 'Ha-ha, Johnny, I got home before you. What took you so long?'"

Johnny's words tore into my heart. Ruth's and my grief was compounded when we discovered how senseless our son's death really was. Nelson didn't die through a car's mechanical failure or by natural causes. Perhaps we could have accepted that. No, Nelson died because someone had not stopped his car for a school bus that was unloading children.

Much to our dismay, the man turned out to be a New York City policeman, a person we thought would know the law about stopping for buses with blinking lights. But he hadn't. Both he and his wife had been taken to the police station, where he had then been arrested. After posting bond, his trial was set for January 17, 1975, three months away.

Why, Ruth and I agonized, *hadn't this man been more careful? Why couldn't he have waited?* The whole thing was so pointless. The more we thought about it, the more it filled us with anguish. And our friends' and neighbors' feelings only seemed to add fuel to our torment.

"I sure hope that guy gets all that's coming to him," a man told me one day in the hardware store.

"You're going to throw the book at him, aren't you?" another asked.

Even the school authorities, hoping to make a case out of stopping for school buses, urged us to press charges.

Ruth and I were beside ourselves. As Christians, we had received the Lord's reassurance that Nelson was now in eternal life. But how, we cried out, were we to deal with the man whose negligence caused us so much heartache?

A few weeks after Nelson's funeral, an insurance adjustor called on us to clear up matters concerning the accident. He mentioned he'd visited the New York couple shortly before.

"They seem broken up," he added.

They're broken up? I thought. What about all the tears we've shed?

Yet a certain curiosity—perhaps a desire for an explanation—led Ruth and me to ask if it would be possible for us to meet with them.

The insurance man looked at us oddly. "You really want to see them?"

"Yes," I said.

He agreed to act as intermediary, and to our surprise, the couple, whose names were Frank and Rose Ann, accepted our invitation to come for dinner the Monday before Thanksgiving.

As the day drew closer, I became more dubious about our decision. Could I really face them again? Why were we putting ourselves up to this?

Ruth and I prayed long and hard about it. Night after night we asked the Lord to provide us with his strength and guidance when they arrived.

When the day came—just a month and a half after our son's death—I looked out the kitchen window to see a car coming up our lane through a light rain. My hand trembled as I reached for the kitchen door to let them in.

We gathered in the living room and the conversation was

forced. After comparing country life to city life, everything we talked about seemed to be an outgrowth of the tragedy.

But in talking with them, I began to notice something strange. A feeling of compassion came over me.

Frank was a policeman who'd been on the force for eight years. He had a spotless record, but the accident, he said, might cost him his job. As a member of the tactical force in a high-crime area of Brooklyn, Frank put his life on the line for others every day. He worked hard at his job, certainly as hard as I did on the farm.

And Rose Ann, like Ruth, had three children at home. She had looked forward to their vacation last October—their first trip away from the city since their marriage. But now she was worried. The New York papers had printed an account of the accident, and because of it, they were staying with Rose Ann's parents, fearful of facing their neighbors.

"I just don't know what's going to happen," Frank said. His eyes, like his wife's, seemed vacant. Both had lost a great deal of weight.

At dinner, we ate quietly. It was while we were having coffee that they noticed a picture that hung on the kitchen wall, a chalk drawing of Jesus and the lost sheep.

"Nelson loved to look at that," Ruth said. "His faith, like ours, was important." She went on to explain how she and I had grown up in a local church and how we both were long-time Sunday-school teachers at our Mennonite church.

"But it's more than a church," Ruth said. "You've really got to live out your beliefs every day."

Frank and Rose Ann nodded. After dinner we drove them around for a while, showing them a wax museum and a schoolhouse, sights they'd meant to see on their first trip here.

After they left, Ruth and I faced each other at the kitchen table. We had suffered, we knew, but surely not as much as that couple was suffering. And the strange thing was, I could now understand their suffering. Frank, like me, was human. Though he came from a different background—a big city that I didn't understand—he was a human being, with all the faults and frailties I had. He had made a mistake that anyone could have made. Jesus Christ was a man too—the Perfect Man—and through him I could see that hatred or vengeance was not the way to handle that mistake—certainly not if Ruth and I professed to live out our faith every day.

Frank and Rose Ann, I could see now, were like those lost sheep in the picture, and that's why they were brought back to our house. Only through Ruth's and my compassion—only through our employing the kind of love Jesus stood for—could we find peace and they find their way home.

Realizing that, on January 17, at the trial, I did not press charges. Except for a traffic fine, Frank was free.

Ruth and I still correspond with the couple. We hope to visit them in New York City someday soon, for we want to see the city, see them again, and meet their three children.

Though Nelson is gone, even in death he continues to teach us something about life. Not long ago I found a little pencil box of his. As I emptied it, a scrap of paper fell out. On it was "Jeremiah 33:3," a verse Nelson was to memorize for a skit. "Call to me and I will answer you and will tell you great and mighty things which you have not known."

I have to believe that Nelson, in his brief life, discovered some of those mighty things, especially the greatness of God's love and how we must spread it around to others.

When Ruth and I called out to God, his message was just as powerful. No matter how deep the wound of sorrow is, forgiveness and faith in God will provide the strength to "occupy till Christ returns" (Luke 19:13), and the broken pieces of our lives will be made whole in him.

His Mysterious Ways

MY HUSBAND, Walt, and I live just down the street from the rectory, so when Father Nuwer caught pneumonia that March, we offered to help in any way we could. We'd be happy to bring him a hot meal, take him to a doctor's appointment—whatever he needed. Walt and I were both retired, so we had plenty of free time.

"Don't hesitate to call on us day or night," Walt told Father Nuwer. "We are always here for you."

We were cleaning up after dinner one evening when the phone rang. It was Father Nuwer.

"I'm having trouble breathing," he said, his voice raspy and strained. "Can you drive me to the hospital?"

"I'll be right over," Walt said. He threw on his coat and shoes and dashed out the door.

Walt got into our car and headed for the rectory. I tried to watch some TV, but I couldn't concentrate on anything; I was too worried. Father Nuwer was asthmatic. I knew that if he had a serious asthma attack on top of his pneumonia, it could kill him.

I stared at the clock, trying to guess when they'd reach the emergency room and how long it would take to see a doctor. Minutes ticked by, then hours. It was nearly eleven P.M. *Why hasn't Walt called?* I wondered. *Is Father Nuwer going to be okay?*

Just as I was about to shut off the TV, the phone rang. I grabbed the receiver.

"Walt?"

But it was my daughter, Donna.

"Don't worry, Mom," she told me. "The hospital just let me know that he's all right."

"Thank goodness," I said. "But why would the hospital call you about Father Nuwer?"

"Father Nuwer?" Donna asked. "He's fine. He must have had the hospital call me first. It's Dad. He had a heart attack. The doctor said that if they hadn't been able to use the defibrillator on him right away, he might not have made it."

Donna paused. "Lucky thing Dad was right there in the emergency room when it happened."

Lucky? I think it was more than that.

— MARY JANE KELSCH, *February 2004*

Pen Pals

MARILYN K. STRUBE

November 1997

*I*n the lunchroom that day, I surreptitiously studied the cool girls, hoping to figure out their secret. Was it their skirts, rolled to mini length? Or their boyfriends, who trotted beside them carrying their books? Mom made me wear my skirts at my knee, and Dad said I wasn't allowed to date until I was sixteen, a whole year away. The other girls at this huge high school always seemed to be surrounded by friends. Meanwhile, I sat alone day after day, my diary my only confidant.

I can't stand being my boring old self anymore, God. Can't you make my life more exciting? With a sigh, I went back to the letter in front of me. At least my eighteen-year-old brother, Dave, appreciated me . . . sort of. He was serving in the Army in Vietnam and wanted me to write to a couple of the guys in his platoon. What could I possibly tell them that would be of any interest?

One of my classmates sauntered past. I thought I heard her

snicker. I hid my burning face behind my hair, and wrote Dave, "Maybe I can see if some of the popular girls will write to your friends."

We heard from Dave that Sunday, one of his infrequent calls from Vietnam. "Mare, don't give my buddies' names to the popular girls," he said. "They used to have girlfriends like them, but they got dumped for guys who are stateside. You always ask if there's something you can do for me. Well, this is it. You write them. Okay?"

That night instead of writing in my diary, I took a sheet of paper from my loose-leaf binder and started a letter: "My name is Marilyn, I'm Dave's sister. But I guess you know that. Ha ha. I like English and art but hate geometry. I feel like my life's on hold. I can't wait to be a grownup. Sorry I don't have anything interesting to write about. P.S. The leaves have turned orange and red. I love crunching through them at the park!"

A few weeks passed. I guess I was too boring to deserve an answer. Then I got two letters.

"My name is Jerry. I know how you feel. I am a grownup, I guess, but my life is on hold too until I go home. Being an adult isn't all it's cracked up to be. Don't be in such a hurry. P.S. We used to make huge piles of leaves and jump in them! I miss autumn bonfires. Thanks for reminding me." Mike's letter was pretty much the same, except he wanted to know what we were having for supper.

Every week I wrote Jerry and Mike, as well as two other guys, Steve and Tom. Now I never seemed to run out of stuff to tell them. I wrote about funny things, and sad things too. "I saw a dead cat today in the woods where our art class went to sketch. I felt so stupid because I started to cry."

The guys told me about the pets they missed back home. Steve added a P.S.: "I used to cry every night when I first came over here. Now I never cry and I wonder what's wrong with me. Be thankful you still cry."

For almost an entire year, from 1968 to 1969, I confided in Steve, Tom, Mike, and Jerry. They wrote me the same way, sharing whatever was on their minds. As awkward as I felt with the kids at school, I felt comfortable talking to these guys I had never even met.

During study hall one day I wrote, "Sister Judith Ann handed out a book called *Who Am I, God?* My mom says, 'You are who your friends are.' My best friend moved away. We used to love to walk to the movies on Sunday afternoons. I haven't made any new friends since I started high school. I guess I'm nobody."

Tom replied, "I like to think I am who I am in spite of my friends! Seriously, a lot of people will want to tell you who you are. Don't let them. It's something you have to figure out for yourself. P.S. I loved movies on Sunday afternoons too! What I'd give for a box of Milk Duds!"

His letter made me feel better. Still, it didn't stop me from wondering as I lay in bed at night, dreading yet another lonely lunch at school, *Who am I, God?* No answer seemed to be forthcoming. I guessed God had more important things to worry about, like the war in Vietnam.

But my classmates seemed pretty clear on who I was: an outsider. It had its advantages. It was easy to observe the different cliques. In each, the kids all thought the same about everything. I just couldn't bring myself to act that way.

That's not to say I didn't want to fit in. I tried to connect with people I knew from grammar school. But they said there wasn't any room left at their lunch table. Another time a group of girls invited me to go to a dance. They seemed kind of tough, but I was grateful to be included. Afterward they wanted to vandalize a cemetery. "No," I said. "I just want to go home." They made fun of me for the rest of the semester. I wrote the guys and asked, "Why am I so weird? Why can't I be like everyone else?"

They answered in one letter, the way they did when they had something really important to tell me. "You're not weird; you're brave. It takes guts to be different." It was nice to know that there were people on my side, even if they were half a world away.

That night I wrote an opinion piece about Vietnam for composition class. It wasn't a difficult assignment because I knew guys who were serving there. What was hard was reading my essay in front of the class the next day. I kept my eyes riveted to my paper. "My brother is there and I write to four guys in his platoon. At first I didn't think I'd have anything to write about, but after a while I found we had lots in common." I quoted from one of Steve's letters: "Some of us enlisted and some of us were drafted. It doesn't much matter anymore how we got here. We just look forward to when we are not."

Surprisingly, my classmates weren't wearing their usual expressions of disdain; they were actually listening. I took a deep breath and concluded, "Maybe instead of war, enemies should be required to be pen pals. I don't know. I'm confused about

Vietnam—and life in general. I just hope the ones who are in power are not."

"You guys should have seen it!" I wrote when I got home. "The class just sat there gaping at me. Then one of the kids got up and started clapping, then another joined him, and then the whole class gave me a standing ovation! My face got really hot but, boy, it was great feeling accepted! P.S. A girl invited me to a party at her house. I used to think she was stuck up, but she's just shy. I bet I've been wrong about a lot of kids. Maybe today they thought the same about me."

I had only had a few days to enjoy my newfound social life when Dad took me aside. "Dave's been injured," he said. "He's going to be okay, but they're sending him home." My brother was coming home!

Then I started trembling. "What about the rest of the guys?" I asked. "Are they coming home too?"

My dad was silent for a moment. When he spoke, his voice sounded strange. "Dave will tell you about it."

He didn't need to. The next day my letter came back, unopened and stamped *Return to Sender*. I stood at the mailbox, tears falling on the envelope and smearing my friends' names. They would never know how they had helped me to become somebody, somebody I had been trying to find for a long time— myself.

Oddly enough, I got a letter from the guys a week later. They had mailed it the day of the deadly ambush. "It won't be long now until our tour of duty is up, and we will be going home. We wanted to tell you goodbye. Thank you for writing us. We don't know if you figured out who you are yet. Sometimes it's just a matter of knowing who you don't want to be. Your brother is a nut. He's always singing Dean Martin's 'You're Nobody, 'Til Somebody Loves You.' If that's true, you definitely are somebody. We all love you."

After school I told Sister Judith Ann about the guys. "I'm sorry," she said. "I know you'll miss them."

I nodded. "Writing them was like writing in a diary that could talk back."

"I have a diary like that," she said. She showed me her Bible. The margins were filled with her handwriting. "I write down my thoughts, and God answers with his Word."

I know he does, because ever since, I have kept a diary like Sister Judith Ann's.

Last summer I visited the Vietnam Veterans Memorial in Washington, D.C. At the wall I found the 1969 section. I kissed my fingertips and touched them to the names etched in the smooth, cold granite. Jerry, Mike, Tom, and Steve were home with God, and I had a feeling that somehow they would get the long-overdue letter that I was writing them in my heart:

"Whenever my life seems on hold, I try to live the in-between moments the way you guys did. You taught me to value ordinary things, like autumn leaves and movies, faithful pets and letters from faraway friends . . . and even what's for supper. These days I write whatever's on my mind in my Bible. God is faithful about listening and answering, just like you guys were. Thanks for believing in me. I love you. P.S. We're having spaghetti tonight."

Donnie and His Van

OSSIE MOBLEY

November 1998

I glanced out the kitchen window as I finished doing the breakfast dishes one Sunday morning last August. My gaze skimmed over the old gas pumps and the Coke machine in front of our little country store, and it lingered on my son, Donnie. He sat in the shade in his wheelchair, waiting for me so we could head across the street to church.

Something about the happy expression on his face took me back to when he was a boy waiting in front of the store for the bus. Every morning he was out there with his best friends, Billy Williams and Bobby Smith, just like he was going to school too. But he never had a chance to go.

Donnie has cerebral palsy due to a brain injury at birth, and during his childhood—in the forties and fifties—there weren't schools nearby for children like him. So he followed with his eyes as the other kids climbed on the bus, one by one. Billy and Bobby yelled goodbye and waved. Donnie watched longingly as the bus rumbled away, staring after it as it seemed to get smaller and smaller down the road, till it disappeared in the distance. It just about broke my heart to see my son hoping for something that would never happen.

Guess it still does, I thought as I put down the dishrag and went out to meet him. Eighty-plus years on this earth had taught me to be practical. There's no point in spending your life wishing for the impossible. You just make the best of what you've got.

That's why for all those years, I had tried to discourage Donnie's request for a van with a wheelchair lift. I would've loved for him to be able to go everywhere with his friends, but there was no way we could afford a luxury like that. Besides, I wouldn't know how to drive it. I had explained the situation to Donnie over and over, and I thought he had finally accepted it.

Then, a few months back, friends of ours rented a van to take us to a concert. Donnie liked riding in it so much that he didn't want to get out when we got home. Ever since, he had been hounding me to ask people at church to help him pray for a van of his own. (He has a hard time speaking, so I usually have to translate.)

He had already told some of his friends. I wasn't about to get the entire congregation involved. They had already given Donnie so much: they built a wheelchair ramp that led to our back door, installed an elevator in the church, and found someone to donate a used computer. It wouldn't be right to ask for more. As good as it made our friends feel to help Donnie, I knew they would feel a thousand kinds of bad when they couldn't come through with a van for him.

I slid into my usual seat in church, close to the elevator, with Donnie beside me in the aisle. I was glad we were sitting in the back when the new youth minister, Brad Charles, announced he was going to take prayer requests. Maybe he wouldn't have time to get to us. But the minute Brad started down the aisle, Donnie opened his mouth. Before I could stop him, his plea rang out: "Aaaaan!"

A hush fell over the congregation. I was so mortified, I couldn't even look at anyone. Brad knelt by Donnie and put his arm around him. One of our friends whispered, "Donnie's been wanting a van with one of those contraptions that can lift his wheelchair."

Brad jumped up like a jack-in-the-box. "Folks, Donnie's believing God for a van," he announced. "Aren't you, Donnie?"

Donnie nodded and laughed, delighted. It was the first real encouragement he had ever gotten about it. "Well, you keep right on praying and believing," Brad said, "and so will we. Nothing's impossible with God!" Then he bowed his head and asked God to send Donnie a van, like it wasn't any big deal.

Donnie smiled all through the rest of the service. I didn't. I knew he was in for the biggest disappointment of his life. *Lord, don't let my boy be hurt.*

After church, Bobby and Billy walked us home as usual. The two of them have stuck by Donnie ever since their bus-stop days. Even though they're busy with their own families—and they've both got grandchildren now—they visit with him nearly every week.

I held my tongue while they were over, but as soon as they left, I lit into Donnie. "That minister is so young, he believes God can do just about anything," I said. "But you! You know as well as I do that things don't always happen the way you want. Vans don't fall out of the sky!"

Donnie shook his head and jutted his chin upward stubbornly. I made out what he was trying to say: "If God wants it to happen . . ."

It was my turn to shake my head.

During the next few months, I tried to put the whole matter behind me. People at church seemed to respect that I didn't want to talk about it, because they didn't bring it up again. But not Donnie. He just wouldn't let up. I don't think a single day went by that he didn't mention a van, only now it had become his van. He even wondered what color it would be!

About the only time he let me have any peace was during worship. By November, I was wishing services would go on twice as long—and it wasn't only because I enjoyed the fellowship. When the service ended the Sunday before Thanksgiving, I followed Billy and Donnie out to the parking lot reluctantly.

Suddenly Billy stopped right in the middle of the lot. Everyone gathered around us and got quiet. I looked at my friends. What was going on?

Then I saw it: A red van with a big bow and a sign that read, "For Donnie Mobley"! One of the church elders handed Donnie the title. "It's all yours."

Donnie threw his head back and looked into the sky. I understood exactly what he was saying, and I reckon all our friends did too: "Thank you, Lord. Thank you!"

Billy pressed some buttons in the van. The lift came out and its mechanical arm gently picked Donnie up in his wheelchair and put him inside the van. A cheer went up from the crowd. Then Billy got behind the wheel. Bobby hopped into the front seat beside him, and the three of them took off, looking as thrilled as teenagers going cruising in their first car.

It turned out that Shirley Shelnutt, a childhood friend of Donnie's, happened to visit our church the day he had made his prayer request. She told Ed and Annie Butchart, directors of Friends of Disabled Adults and Children in Stone Mountain, Georgia. Not long after, someone called the Butcharts to donate a van equipped with a wheelchair lift; it only needed to be towed in for some minor repairs. Then Jack Gibson volunteered the use of his towing service. Robert and Johnny Palmer, who own an auto salvage place down the road from us, got the van running. Our neighbor Peggy Smith paid the insurance. She and Doug and Judy Ross had the chair hitch replaced. Billy, Bobby, and other folks said I wouldn't have to worry about learning to drive the van; they'd be happy to take Donnie anywhere he wanted.

And they do. In the past year he's gone to see the Christmas lights in town, to the mall, to concerts, to ball games. I'm hardly the sentimental type, but I must confess that every time I see Donnie drive off with his friends, it gives my heart a lift. I follow his van down the road with my eyes until it disappears in the distance, and I think, *Why not spend your life hoping for the best? If God wants it to happen . . .*

The Courage to
Make a Difference

The Test of a Man

THOMAS J. FLEMING

August 1966

I can still hear my father telling the story about old Mr. Blaine and his watch factory:

"We went to work as soon as we got out of grammar school in those days," he would begin. "Most of the kids my age worked in a watch factory next door to where we lived. It was assembly line work, dull as dishwater. But we were paid a dollar a day—good money in 1900.

"Each morning they opened the doors, and we filed in one by one. Sitting there behind a desk would be an old high-collared clerk. You'd get in front of the desk and he'd ask, 'Protestant or Catholic?'

"If someone answered 'Catholic,' he was told, 'No openings today.' If you said 'Protestant,' you were handed a slip and told to report to a certain section for work. Like many other Catholics in the line, I gritted my teeth and said 'Protestant.' We needed the buck that badly."

The simple brutality of this story awoke a fierce anger in my boyish mind, and I understood why my father had joined Frank Hague and his political cohorts in the 1920s. I never tired of hearing how they had battled the ruling class for power in Jersey City.

Galled by years of injustice from men like Blaine, they had built an aggressive political machine that stormed out of the slums and took charge of the city.

I was no longer surprised to learn that they did not fight with kid gloves, but rather they fought at the ballot box. They were bitter, they were tough, and some of them were mean. I understood why.

As I grew older, I realized my father was an unusual politician in many ways. Money meant little to him. He was never especially interested in the easy life it could buy. My father spent ninety percent of his time doing the invisible part of the local politician's job. If the Zaretskis and their five children were freezing in an unheated house, he paid for a ton of coal, no questions asked. When Rose Klinger and her children, deserted by her husband, were literally starving, groceries would be delivered within the hour.

Paternalism? Of course. I am not recommending it, but to the immigrant poor of my father's era, it made all the difference to know that the men in power cared about the quality of their daily lives. Their response at the ballot box changed the city forever.

After one final titanic battle in which both sides used every trick in the political books, the old ruling class bitterly admitted defeat and all but abandoned their attempts to regain control of the city. Many of them sold their factories and left the city. Others chose to barricade themselves within a small, purely social world, and invest their family money in the stock market.

Then came 1929. None of these first families was ultra-rich.

Hundreds of them were practically wiped out by the stock market's catastrophic plunge. Reduced to genteel poverty, they moldered in their big houses, and as the Depression lengthened, these too decayed.

One of these mansions was only a block away from our home. Surrounded by uncut hedges and a weedy lawn, it looked like something out of a Charles Addams' cartoon. We kids called it "the haunted house."

One day I happened to mention the house to my father. He laughed and said, "It isn't haunted—except maybe by memories. I know the family well. They used to own that watch factory where I worked when I was your age.

"Only Blaine's son is left now," my father continued. "A musician. From what I understand, he lost every cent he had in the crash."

The Depression years ground away, reducing all opposition to the Hague regime to near invisibility. But the test of a man is not simply his ability to acquire money and power—it is what he does with these things. One winter night in the early 1940s, I saw my father meet this test. Out of the haunted house came the scion of the old watch factory owner. Up the street he came to ring our bell and ask to see my father.

For a moment my father looked startled when I told him who was waiting for him in the living room. Then a more serious, thoughtful expression passed over his face. "Tell him I'll be right down," he said.

He finished dressing with his usual meticulous care. I stood in the doorway, trying to read some emotion on his face. I realized a kind of climax to an ancient bitterness was about to be enacted downstairs.

From a vantage point on the stairway, I watched and listened as my father strode into the living room to confront his visitor.

"Nice to see you, Mr. Blaine," he said, holding out his hand. "What can I do for you?"

Mr. Blaine seemed surprised by the extended hand. He seized it awkwardly, then sat down on the edge of the couch. His cuffs were frayed, and there was a stain on the sleeve of his coat. He fingered his hat for a long moment, then blurted, "Mr. Fleming, I need a job. I don't know whether you can help me. I don't know whether you will help me. I know my family hasn't been on your side politically."

There was silence for a moment. Here, if ever, was the perfect moment for revenge. How easily my father could even the score for those days of humiliation in the watch factory by throwing this man out of our house. In the same racing moment in which my mind gathered in all the possibilities, I realized with a shock that I wanted him to do just that. In the most savage, burning way, I wanted to savor the taste of revenge. "Now ask him, 'Protestant or Catholic?'" I wanted to scream.

Instead, I heard my father's voice, steady and calm. "What kind of work can you do, Mr. Blaine?"

"Well, I'm an organist, but these days most churches don't have enough money to pay a salary," Blaine replied.

My father knew little about church organists and their demand. He went to church and had a strong faith, though he seldom talked about it. He just lived it.

"You're a college graduate, aren't you?" Dad continued.

"Yes, of course."

"Ever work in a library?"

"No."

"But you know your way around books?"

"Yes. Yes, I think I do."

"How would you like a job as a city librarian?"

"Mr. Fleming, that would be—just perfect."

"I heard about an opening. I'll see what I can do." My father stood up and held out his hand once more. "I'll call you tomorrow."

Blaine shook his hand. "Mr. Fleming, I can't thank you enough. . . ."

Blaine did not realize it, of course, but when he shook my father's hand he was sealing a bargain. In the tough code of the city's politicians, a handshake was an absolute contract. Many times I had seen men ask my father for favors, and he would refuse to shake hands with them because he was not sure he could deliver on his promise. Shaking this man's hand meant he would go down to City Hall tomorrow morning and battle other politicians who also had candidates for that librarian job.

Mr. Blaine disappeared into the windy night. I sat on the stairs thinking of those ragged lines filing into the watch factory each morning to accept their humiliation. But they no longer brought up a destructive bitterness or a defeating hatred inside me. They were part of history now—a foolish, sad history. With five minutes of matter-of-fact kindness, my father had healed the wound.

Where Healing Begins

BUD WELCH

May 1999

The floor shook beneath my feet. I ran to the kitchen window. I saw blue sky, spring sunshine. Just a peaceful Oklahoma day. It was hard to imagine anything terrible happening on a bright Wednesday like that. I hadn't put on my Texaco uniform that morning; I was meeting my twenty-three-year-old daughter, Julie, for lunch. Was I proud of her? Everyone who came in for an oil change heard what a great kid I had. She'd caught me bragging on her just two days before. "Dad! People don't want to hear all that!"

Odd, that visit . . . Julie often stopped by my service station for a few minutes on her way home from her job at the Murrah Building in downtown Oklahoma City. (Her mother and I were divorced.) Monday, though, it was as if . . . she didn't want to leave. She stayed two hours, then threw her arms around me. Julie always gave me a hug when she left, but Monday she held me a long time.

"Goodbye, Daddy," she'd said.

That was odd too. Nowadays Julie only called me Daddy when she had something really important to say. Well, maybe she'd tell me about it that afternoon. Every Wednesday I met Julie for lunch at the Athenian restaurant across from the Murrah Building.

At nine o'clock I'd sat down with that cup of coffee to wait for her call. Julie usually got to work at the Social Security office where she was a translator at 8:00 A.M. sharp. It was her first job after college. As a federal employee, Julie got only thirty minutes for lunch—and she wouldn't take thirty-one! She always called to find out what I wanted for lunch, then phoned our order in to the Athenian so we could eat as soon as we arrived.

Chicken sandwich this time, I'd decided. The parking lot would be full by lunchtime; I'd see Julie's red Pontiac in her favorite spot beneath a huge old American elm tree. I'd park my truck at one of the meters on the street and watch for her to come out of the big glass doors. She was such a little person, just five feet tall ("Five feet, one-half inch, Dad!"), 103 pounds.

But she had a big heart. I believed in loving your neighbor and all the rest I heard in church on Sundays. But Julie! She lived her faith all day, every day. She spent her free time helping the needy. She taught Sunday school and volunteered for Habitat for Humanity. I kidded her that she was trying to save the whole world single-handedly.

The rumbling subsided. Bewildered, I stood staring out the kitchen window. Then the phone rang. I grabbed it.

"Julie?"

It was my brother Frank, calling from his car on his way out to the family farm where we'd grown up. "Is your TV on, Bud? Radio says there's been an explosion downtown."

Downtown? Eight miles away? What kind of explosion could rock my table way out here? On the local news channel, I saw an aerial view of downtown from the traffic helicopter. Through clouds of smoke and dust, the camera zoomed in on a nine-story building with its entire front half missing. An announcer's voice said, ". . . the Alfred P. Murrah Federal Building . . ."

The screen showed floors thrusting straight out into space. Tangled wreckage in rooms with no outer wall. And in place of those big glass doors, a mountain of rubble three stories high.

I didn't move. I scarcely breathed. My world stopped at that moment. They were appealing for people not to come into the downtown area, but nothing could have pulled me away from the telephone anyway. Julie would be calling. Her office was at the back of the building, the part still standing. Julie would find her way to a phone and dial my number.

All that day, all that night, all the next day and night, I sat by the phone, while relatives and friends fanned out to every hospital. Twice the phone rang with the news that Julie's name was on a survivor's list! Twice it rang again with a correction: The lists were not of survivors, but simply of people who worked in the building.

Friday morning, two days after the explosion, I gave up my sleepless vigil and drove downtown. Because I had a family member still missing, police let me through the barricade. Cranes, search dogs, and an army of rescue workers toiled among hills of rubble—one of them a mound of debris that had been the

Athenian restaurant. Mangled automobiles, Julie's red Pontiac among them, surrounded a scorched and broken elm tree, its new spring leaves stripped away like so many bright lives.

Julie, where are you? Rescuers confirmed that everyone else working in that rear office had made it out alive. The woman at the desk next to Julie's had come away with only a cut on her arm. But at exactly 9:00 A.M., Julie had left her desk and walked to the reception room up front, to escort her first two clients back to her office.

They found the three bodies Saturday morning in the corridor, a few feet from safety.

From the moment I learned it was a bomb—a premeditated act of murder—that had killed Julie and 167 others, from babies in their cribs to old folks applying for their pensions, I survived on hate. When Timothy McVeigh and Terry Nichols were arrested, I seethed at the idea of a trial. Why should those monsters live another day?

Other memories blur together . . . Julie's college friends coming from all over the country to her funeral. Victims' families meeting. Laying flowers on my daughter's grave. No time frame for any of it. For me, time was stuck at 9:02 A.M., April 19, 1995.

One small event did stand out among the meaningless days. One night—two months after the bombing? four months?—I was watching a TV update on the investigation, fuming at the delays, when the screen showed a stocky, gray-haired man stooped over a flower bed. "Cameramen in Buffalo today," a reporter said, "caught a rare shot of Timothy McVeigh's father in his . . ."

I sprang to the set. I didn't want to see this man, didn't want to know anything about him. But before I could switch it off, the man looked up, straight at the camera. It was only a glimpse of his face, but in that instant I saw a depth of pain like . . .

Like mine.

Oh, dear God, I thought, *this man has lost a child too.*

That was all, a momentary flash of recognition. And yet that face, that pain, kept coming back to me as the months dragged on, my own pain unchanged, unending.

January 1996 arrived, a new year on the calendar, but not for me. I stood at the cyclone fence around the cleared site of the Murrah Building, as I had so often in the previous nine months. The fence held small remembrances: a teddy bear, a photograph, a flower.

My eyes traveled past the mementos to the shattered elm tree where Julie had always parked. The tree was bare on that January day, but in my mind I saw it as it had looked the summer after the bombing. Incredibly, impossibly, those stripped and broken branches had thrust out new leaves.

The thought that came to me then seemed to have nothing to do with new life. It was the sudden, certain knowledge that McVeigh's execution would not end my pain. The pain was there to stay. The only question was what I would let it do to me.

Julie, you wouldn't know me now! Angry and bitter, hate cutting me off from Julie's way of love, from Julie herself. There in front of me, inside that cyclone fence, was what blind hate had brought about. The bombing on the anniversary of the Branch Davidian deaths in Waco, Texas, was supposed to avenge what McVeigh's obsessed mind believed was a government wrong. I knew something about obsession now; I knew what brooding on a wrong can do to your heart.

I looked again at the tenacious old elm that had survived the worst that hate could do. And I knew that in a world where wrongs are committed every day, I could do one small thing, make one individual decision, to stop the cycle.

Many people didn't understand when I quit publicly agitating for McVeigh's execution. A reporter, interviewing victims' families on the first anniversary of the bombing, heard about my change of heart and mentioned it in a story that went out on the wire services. I began to get invitations to speak to various groups. One invitation, in the fall of 1998, three years after the bombing, came from a nun in Buffalo. Buffalo . . . what had I heard about that place? Then I remembered. Tim McVeigh's father.

Reach out. To the father of Julie's killer? Maybe Julie could have, but not me. Not to this guy. That was asking too much.

Except Julie couldn't reach out now.

The nun sounded startled when I asked if there was some way I could meet Mr. McVeigh. But she called back to say she'd contacted his church. He would meet me at his home Saturday morning, September 5.

That is how I found myself ringing the doorbell of a small yellow frame house in upstate New York. It seemed a long wait before the door opened and the man whose face had haunted me for three years looked out.

"Mr. McVeigh?" I asked. "I'm Bud Welch."

"Let me get my shoes on," he said.

He disappeared and I realized I was shaking. What was I

doing here? What could we talk about? The man emerged with his shoes on and we stood there awkwardly.

"I hear you have a garden," I said finally. "I grew up on a farm."

We walked to the back of the house, where neat rows of tomatoes and corn showed a caring hand. For half an hour we talked weeds and mulch—we were Bud and Bill now—then he took me inside and we sat at the kitchen table drinking ginger ale. Family photos covered a wall. He pointed out pictures of his older daughter, her husband, his baby granddaughter. He saw me staring at a photo of a good-looking boy in suit jacket and tie. "Tim's high school graduation," he said simply.

"Gosh," I exclaimed, "what a handsome kid!"

The words were out before I could stop them. Any more than Bill could stop the tears that filled his eyes.

His younger daughter, Jennifer, twenty-four years old, came in, hair damp from the shower. Julie never got to be twenty-four, but I knew right away the two would have hit it off. Jennifer had just started teaching at an elementary school, her first job too. Some of the parents, she said, had threatened to take their kids out when they saw her last name.

Bill talked about his job on the night shift at a General Motors plant. Just my age, he'd been there thirty-six years. We were two blue-collar joes, trying to do right by our kids. I stayed nearly two hours, and when I got up to leave Jennifer hugged me like Julie always had. We held each other tight, both of us crying. I don't know about Jennifer, but I was thinking that I'd gone to church all my life and had never felt as close to God as I did at that moment.

"We're in this together," I told Jennifer and her dad, "for the rest of our lives. We can't change the past, but we have a choice about the future."

Bill and I keep in touch by telephone, two guys doing our best. What that best will be, neither of us knows, but that broken elm tree gives me a hint. They were going to bulldoze it when they cleared away the debris; but I spearheaded a drive to save the tree, and now it will be part of a memorial to the bomb victims. It may still die, damaged as it is. But we've harvested enough seeds and shoots from it that new life can one day take its place. Just like the seed of caring that Julie left behind, one person reaching out to another. It's a seed that can be planted wherever a cycle of hate leaves an open wound in God's world.

A Place for Mike

BETH ANTHONY

July 1999

I'd just walked into the cafeteria, into the sea of noise that dozens of elementary-school kids with their lunch trays make, when a keening cry pierced the din. A small boy was curled up underneath an empty table, pounding the floor with his fists and wailing inconsolably.

"What in the world is going on?" I asked another teacher. In my fifteen years of teaching in North Charleston's toughest, poorest neighborhoods, I'd come across plenty of troubled students. But I had never seen a child behaving like that!

"No big deal. It's only Mike Woodson," the teacher replied. "He acts out a lot. We just let him go until he settles down."

The Woodson kids. I'd heard all about the seven of them, even though I had started working at the school only a few weeks earlier. "Problems at home, problems in the classroom," I'd been told. "Especially Mike. No one knows what to do with him."

But somebody has to do something! my mind protested as I

looked at the boy huddled on the floor, his face blotched with tears.

The next thing I knew, I was peering under the table. "Hey, Mike? I'm Mrs. Anthony. I'm new here and I need your help." He eyed me warily, his cries subsiding into sniffles. "Could you show me the way to the parking lot? I left some papers in my car."

Mike stared at me, surprised. Abruptly, he crawled out and got to his feet. Standing there in his battered sneakers, wiping his nose, he seemed timid, vulnerable—not at all the troublemaker I'd been warned about. "I'm kind of chicken about new places," I said. "Would you mind holding my hand?"

After a second's hesitation, he stuck his hand in mine and held on tight. As we walked out to my car, I looked at him more closely. His skin and clothes were encrusted with grime.

I got my papers and escorted him to his first-grade class-room. "Thank you for your help, Mike," I said. His hand lingered in mine for a moment before he let go, a shy smile tugging at his lips. Unexpectedly I felt an answering tug on my heart. *This little boy needs so much,* I thought sadly. *More than I can give.*

The next several weeks were busy ones. Yet I couldn't get Mike out of my mind. I kept remembering the sweetness of his smile, the way his warm little hand felt in mine.

Just after spring break we got word at school that the Woodsons' trailer had burned to a charred shell. That evening I told my husband, Jimmy, and our two children what had happened. When I said teachers were rounding up clothes for Mike's family, my kids volunteered to go through their closets.

The next morning I was in the school office dropping off our bag when I heard the secretary address a woman as Mrs. Woodson. She looked too young to be the mother of seven; at the same time, her face was drawn and defeated. "You must be Mike's mom," I said. "I'm sorry about the fire. Is there anything I can do?"

"I've got help with my kids, but . . . Mike's not my son. He's my sister's boy," she explained wearily. "Can you take him tonight?"

It wasn't school policy, but it wasn't against the rules either. This was an emergency. Jimmy and the kids wouldn't mind. "Sure, I'll look after him," I said, pushing back the questions that were speeding through my head.

That afternoon I picked Mike up at his classroom. "Your aunt has her hands full right now. How about coming home with me for the night?" He didn't say anything, just nodded and looked at me with those melted-chocolate eyes.

"Put on your seat belt," I said when we got in the car. Mike didn't move, but I could sense him quivering with tension, as if he might break down any second. "Mike, put on—" Then I noticed his brow furrow in bewilderment. "You've never used a seat belt before?" I guessed, showing him how to buckle up. He had no idea what to do with the straw either when I got him a can of soda on the way to my house.

At home my daughter, Tecla, eleven, and son, Cain, nine, had questions of their own. "Mom, he doesn't have on any socks," Cain said. "You had to show him how to put soap on a washcloth. What's wrong with him?" Tecla asked, "Why doesn't he talk?"

"Mike's been through a rough time," I told them. "Let's make him feel at home."

At dinner Tecla and Cain did their best not to stare as Mike, without a word, wolfed down three servings of sausages and potato nuggets. It helped that Jimmy patted Mike's shoulder and went on chatting with the kids as if his behavior were nothing out of the ordinary.

Later Cain offered to let Mike bunk with him. I was so proud of my son. Mike took everything in with big eyes. I tucked the boys in and announced as usual, "Prayer time."

To my surprise Mike knew what that meant. He crunched his hands together and squeezed his eyes shut intently as I began to pray. "God, please watch over Mike and Cain," I asked. "Let them have a good night's sleep."

The next morning when we got to school, Mike and I ran into his aunt. "Here he is," I said.

Exhaustion was etched on her face. "I've got my own kids to worry about," she said. "Just because my sister can't take care of her boy doesn't mean I have to." She walked off.

"Where do I go after school?" Mike whispered anxiously.

"Why don't you come home with me again," I said, squeezing his hand. It was an incredibly rash offer, maybe even unwise, but I couldn't let this little boy be abandoned. Not again.

At lunch I called my husband and explained the situation. "Oh, Jimmy, maybe I shouldn't have . . ."

"You had to," he assured me. "We'll figure something out."

That night when the kids were asleep—Mike in Cain's room again—Jimmy and I discussed what to do. I was determined to find Mike's relatives. With information I got from his aunt, I managed to track down his mother a few days later. She begged me to keep her son. "Just till I get on my feet. Please? I've got troubles of my own."

But two weeks went by and we didn't hear from her. Mike was an ideal guest, well-behaved, quiet, eager to pitch in with chores. He got along with my kids, although he stuck close to me as if he were afraid I might disappear. Still, Jimmy and I believed it would be better for him to be with his own flesh and blood. I called his aunt. "Even if you can't take him, isn't there someone in your family who can?"

"No," she said sadly. Then she pleaded, "Keep him a little longer. I'm looking for another place."

"I'll have to discuss it with my husband," I said, frustrated.

I talked to Jimmy and laid out my concerns. I was afraid Mike was getting too attached to us, yet I hated the thought of uprooting him again and placing him in foster care. He was way behind developmentally. Mike was eight, but still in first grade because he couldn't read or write. Even his conversational skills were limited. He'd have to have special tutoring. "Oh, Jimmy, I'm worried we won't be able to give him what he needs."

My husband looked at me thoughtfully. "Mike's happy here. I think what he needs right now is to be with us." I hugged Jimmy, grateful he'd been able to help allay my doubts.

"Maybe that's what God wants for him." I said. I'd been asking for the Lord's help all along to find a solution. Maybe this was it.

Once we committed to letting Mike stay with us as long as necessary, everyone seemed to breathe a little easier. Tecla and Cain were amazingly mature about having another kid around. Before long, they were spending their afternoons teaching Mike how to ride Cain's bike. The day he coasted down the driveway, shouting to me gleefully, "Look, Mama, I can do it!" my kids cheered even louder than I did.

The longer Mike stayed with us, the harder it became for us not to fall for this little boy who was so appreciative and so eager to soak up everything. But other people thought we were misguided. "A black kid in a white family? You're asking for trouble," one of my relatives declared. "If you want another child, why don't you find one who looks like you?"

That exchange with my relative aroused my doubts. *Lord, are we really doing the right thing? Would Mike be better off with another family? He needs so much attention. Am I being fair to him? To my own kids?*

Then, six months after Mike came to live with us, we ran into a few of his cousins at a pizza place. That got him hankering to be with his family again, and with his father in particular. I took Mike to the address his aunt gave us in a run-down section of the city. The man reeked of liquor, and it was only when Mike insisted he wanted to stay that I reluctantly assented. I could hardly tear my eyes from his image in the rearview mirror.

That night when I told them that Mike had gone, Tecla and Cain were distraught. "He's not coming back?" my daughter exclaimed.

Cain pleaded, "Can't you do something, Mom?"

I tried to explain. "Remember how I said Mike needed to stay with us for a while? Maybe it's time for him to be with his family."

"But I thought he was part of our family too!" Cain protested.

So did I, I told God. *Now I'm as confused as my kids are.*

Mike's aunt called early the next morning. "I've got Mike. He slept on the street last night! That man can't take care of him. You're the only one who can. Will you take him back?"

She didn't even have to ask.

Mike was subdued for a day or two, then things went back to normal. That episode got me thinking, though: He needed to spend time with other black children and stay in touch with where he came from.

When school ended I signed Mike up for a city-sponsored day camp. He was excited about going the first day. But when I went to pick him up that afternoon, he pulled away and refused to take my hand. He scurried ahead of me to the car.

"What's wrong, darlin'?" I asked as we drove home.

Staring out the window, Mike mumbled, "Everyone wanted to know why a white lady was driving me."

The scene repeated itself the next afternoon. On the third day, Mike walked beside me as we left the building. "It's okay, Mama," he said cheerfully. "I told them you were my baby-sitter, and my mom's at work."

That evening I called the camp director and asked if I might speak to the kids. The following afternoon I sat with Mike at my side before a curious audience, feeling more nervous than I had on my very first day in front of a class. "Once when Mike was learning to ride a bike, he fell down and skinned his knee," I began. "I was cleaning the scrape when he said, 'Look, our blood is the same color!' The color of our skin might be different, but underneath, we're alike.

"I think God brought Mike into our family to show us that what's on the outside isn't important as long as we love each other on the inside." It was becoming clearer to me as I explained it. "I love Mike and he loves me. That's what makes him my son. That's what really matters."

Suddenly, there in front of all the kids in the day camp, Mike reached out and grabbed my hand. Like the first time we'd connected back in the school cafeteria, I felt that unforgettable warmth flowing between us.

Only now I understood it came from God. From the very beginning, he'd been drawing us beyond neglect and prejudice, beyond my doubts and worries, drawing us together with love. And that, in the end, was what Mike, like all of us, needed most.

It Starts with Me

CRAIG KIELBURGER

November 1999

I usually read the comics in the *Toronto Star* each morning before I go to school. But one day in April 1995, a front-page story stopped me. There was a picture of a smiling boy, his arm upraised. His name was Iqbal Masih. He looked to be about my age at the time—twelve. According to the article, he had worked in a carpet factory in Pakistan for most of his life. Then he escaped and traveled in his country and the West, speaking out against child labor. The previous Sunday he had been shot dead by an unknown assailant.

My dog, Muffin, chewed on her scrap of rawhide; Mom poured milk over my cereal; but suddenly everything seemed terribly still. *Why was this kid murdered?* I wondered. *Why did he have to work in a factory?* The most my parents asked of me was to take out the garbage, mow the lawn and get good grades. My cereal went soggy as I read on. I never got to the comics that morning.

All through the school day, I couldn't stop thinking about

Iqbal. Here I was memorizing algebraic formulas while somewhere kids were tying wool into tiny knots from dawn to dusk. How would I have handled it if I were in their place? The article had said Iqbal's parents, who were extremely poor, had sent him to work in the factory when he was just four. Some suspected that factory owners, angry at Iqbal for exposing their abuses, might be behind his killing.

I went to the library and looked for information on child labor practices. Most of the articles were about the often terrible conditions in Europe and North America in the early part of the century. What about nowadays?

One of my mom's friends said I should call human rights organizations. The people I spoke to gave me vague answers. I kept thinking, *Isn't there anything I can do? Why don't they take me seriously? Because I'm twelve?*

Then I heard about a group called Youth Action Network. I called and spoke to Alam Rahman, a recent college graduate. His father had immigrated to Canada from Bangladesh. "If things had been a little bit different," he said, "I could have been a child laborer."

So could I, I thought. If I'd been born in an earlier time or if my family had been poor, it could have been me denied the chance to get an education.

"I think there should be a children's organization fighting child labor," I said. "Kids speaking for kids."

"That's a great idea, Craig. Why don't you start one?"

Me? Sure, I'd helped my older brother, Marc, with his high-school environmental campaigns before he went away to college.

I'd won public speaking competitions, and I had even spoken before the city council on behalf of the local library. But this time I had to convince my classmates. Would they think I was weird? All I knew was I had to do something. Iqbal had been silenced, but I would tell others his story. He deserved that much.

The next day in homeroom, I passed around copies of the article and told the class what I'd learned. On their faces was the same shock that I had felt when I first read the article. "I still don't really know much about it," I admitted, "but I thought maybe some of us could get together and see if there's anything we can do. Who's interested?" A dozen hands shot up.

We dug around for more information and met at my house that evening. As we talked about child labor, I felt this intense connection—both to my classmates and to the kids on whose behalf we had come together. One of the clippings told of a rally of over 250 children in Delhi, India. "Free the children," they had chanted. We would take up their cry. Our group now had a name.

FTC put together youth fair displays and spoke at schools and churches. We did a lot of research, using a fax machine and the Internet to get firsthand accounts of child labor from kids all over the world. We sent petitions to foreign governments, including one with three thousand names to India, urging the release of political prisoner Kailash Satyarthi, a leading crusader against child labor.

Still, we had to fight for respect from many adults. "They ought to be enjoying their childhood instead of wasting it," I once overheard a teacher say. "They're just seventh graders who think they can solve all the world's problems."

Every time a remark like that got to me, I'd think of Iqbal. The carpet factory owners he'd spoken out against had threatened him, and he had lost his life. How could I let myself be intimidated merely by snide comments? The more people doubted us, the more committed we became to proving children could make a difference. We resolved FTC would always be made up only of kids.

We organized a garage sale that summer to raise money for our projects, as well as for overseas organizations fighting for our cause. We got customers to sign our petitions. When it was all over, we'd collected hundreds of dollars and names.

My parents had been incredibly tolerant of all the late-night phone calls and traffic in our house since I'd started FTC. But finally they took me aside. "Next month you'll be starting eighth grade," my mother said. "We're proud of all you've accomplished, but maybe it's time to put FTC behind you." After all, they said, I was advocating kids' right to an education, yet I was working long hours myself.

"I know you think this is just a phase," I told them, "but I've thought and prayed about it a lot, and I really believe I have to do this." The world seemed smaller than it had five months earlier, and for the first time I truly saw myself as part of it.

By the time school started again, FTC had something of a reputation. Some kids resented our opposition to brand-name sneakers and jeans made by child laborers. "Do you want us to make our own clothes? Isn't that child labor?" one boy cracked.

Kids were skeptical of the articles I showed them about child labor. "How do you know all this is true?" a tenth-grade girl asked. "Have you seen these kids for yourself?"

"No, but I hope to someday," I replied weakly. But when? Did I really have any business being a spokesperson for kids I'd never met?

Then one day Alam told me he was planning to spend a year in Asia visiting relatives and traveling. "I'll take you along—this could be your chance to meet some of the workers." My parents trusted and respected Alam. But they didn't even allow me to ride the subway to downtown Toronto by myself. They wanted detailed explanations of Alam's itinerary, whom I would meet, what safety precautions we would take. I e-mailed contacts around the world, hoping for offers of accommodations. Soon the responses started rolling in, asking when I was coming. My parents were being won over.

That fall, I was invited to speak at a convention of the Ontario Federation of Labor, my largest audience ever. I was a nervous wreck, an eighth grader speaking to over two thousand adults. But I started with the story of Iqbal, and soon I found my voice. When I finished there was silence. Then the room exploded in applause.

"We'd like to pledge five thousand dollars to your cause," an OFL spokesperson announced. He handed me a T-shirt and raised my arm in the air. Another organization pledged money, then another. I just stood there with a giant grin on my face, knowing somewhere Iqbal was smiling too. By the end of the night, we had raised a staggering $150,000 to build a rehabilitation center and schools for freed child laborers.

Later, over pizza and pop, my friends and I talked about the future. FTC had become bigger than us—it was a real organization. There was no going back.

I think my parents realized it too. We finalized plans for my trip to Asia. I arranged to take nearly two months off from school. Lying in bed the night before I left, I stared at the poster on my wall of the Chinese proverb, "The journey of a thousand miles begins with a single step." There had been many steps over the previous eight months, all leading up to this journey of ten thousand miles. *God,* I prayed, *please be with me as I take my next big step.*

I left home on December 10, and joined Alam in Dhaka, Bangladesh. I wanted to meet as many working kids as I could. In Tamil Nadu, India, we talked to parents whose children had been killed or crippled in explosions at a fireworks factory. In Bangkok, Thailand, we saw very young kids being exploited in the sex trade. I talked to ten-year-old boys who had quit school to work fifteen-hour days to help support their families, and I realized how frivolous my hours spent playing ball would seem to them.

"It's easy to tell these countries that these kids should not have to work under such horrible conditions," a Western relief agency official told me. "But remember, a big part of the problem is us. We buy this stuff. Instead of merely being a market for these products, the West needs to help find solutions to the underlying poverty in the Third World."

He was right. I came from a society that prided itself on material wealth. I thought of all the video games piled on my desk, the clothes in my closet. Was I part of the problem too?

In Pakistan I talked to a boy making bricks. He had been sold into labor by his grandfather to pay a debt. "Would you like to go to school?" I asked him.

"What is school?" he asked me.

All around me I saw the poverty that drove people to such desperation. I figured the choice was pretty clear in many cases: work or starve.

I had read so much about child laborers, and yet face-to-face, I was amazed at how many were lively, spirited kids. They weren't waiting for anyone to save them. They were making the best of conditions that would devastate most adults.

I also met plenty of young people in school and former child laborers who were determined to make things better for kids who weren't as fortunate. They were dealing with this problem years before I even heard about it, I thought. I told them kids in the West cared too, and we exchanged ideas about what we could do.

But it was the working children I met who made the biggest impact on me. We found a girl with a ribbon in her hair in a run-down building in Madras, India. With no protection for her hands, she was taking apart used syringes so the plastic could be recycled. "Sometimes I cut myself," she said, "but I always wash with water."

I wanted to take her with me. But a woman came in and told us that if the girl's boss found her talking to us, she would be punished.

We had to leave her behind.

What's the point of all this, God? I wondered. *I keep meeting suffering kids and I can't do anything for them.*

Then in Varanasi, India, we were contacted by Kailash Satyarthi, the man whose release FTC had petitioned for months earlier. He had been let go, and recently he had led a raid on a carpet factory, setting free twenty-two children. He invited us to help see them safely home.

We crammed into two Jeeps. The boy next to me was about eight and his name was Munnilal. "I was given no money by my master," he told me. "I was hit again and again." The Jeep jostled as we drove down into a creek. Then it got stuck in the mud. Everyone jumped out and pushed it. When we reached shore, I stood there, exhausted and soaking wet. Munnilal took a blanket from around his shoulders and held it out to me. "Here, you'll catch cold," he said.

"No, you keep it," I said, staring at this child who had been through more hardship in eight years than I would ever go through. In that instant, I understood. Munnilal had almost nothing, but what he had, he offered me. For most of the kids I met, all I could do was share their stories and raise money, but I would do it as sincerely as Munnilal had offered me that blanket.

We got back in the Jeeps and drove the children to their villages, stopping to watch each reunion. When Munnilal's mother saw him, she hugged him, weeping. "You are so thin," she said.

"When I hurt most," he said to her, "I saw you in my dreams."

"I saw you in my dreams too," she answered.

I thought of my mom waiting for my calls, the way she was marking off each day of my trip on the calendar. Suddenly I felt terribly homesick.

But there was one more stop to make, the one that I had thought about most. In Muridke, Pakistan, we walked down the route of Iqbal's funeral procession. "The day Iqbal died, a thousand other Iqbals were born," a girl had said at his funeral. I was grateful to be one of them.

As I stood before his unmarked grave, I thought back to the story about him that changed my life. The world had come into a new focus that day. I saw lots of injustice, but I also saw how to change it. It starts with me—with each one of us, with what we can do to make things better. I took the first step of my journey because of Iqbal, but I continue it because of kids like Munnilal and the little girl in Madras. No, maybe I can't solve all the world's problems. But I can work to solve some, with the help of other kids—and grownups—who care and a God who guides us all.

His Mysterious Ways

HURRYING THROUGH THE SUPERMARKET, I knocked over a display of shoelaces. In my embarrassment, I flung one packet into the cart and, after paying, tossed it into my purse. Then I was off to the rehabilitation hospital where I'd been visiting Donald, a man whose arms and legs were paralyzed after he'd fallen from a ladder.

That day Donald was unusually despondent. "Brenda," he said, "Sometimes I feel as though God simply doesn't care anymore."

"You know he cares," I began. But I had no real answer for him. We sat in silence.

"Oh, by the way," Donald said as I started to leave, "the nurse broke one of my shoestrings. Could you get me a new pair?"

I opened my purse and took out the packet from the supermarket. We stared at the shoestrings in amazement. I laced them into Donald's shoes.

Shoestrings! For a pair of shoes on feet that could not move to wear them out. For a set of hands that couldn't even tie the bow.

"Donald, if God cares enough to supply you with shoestrings

even before you ask," I said, "I'm certain he cares enough about you in more important ways."

A smile broke onto his face. "Yes, you're right," Donald said. "I'm sure too."

Shoestrings. Whenever I'm discouraged, I think of them. Then I know that God cares for me too. Right down to the laces in my shoes.

—BRENDA MINNER, *December 1981*

Trusting in God

Free Ice Water

TED HUSTEAD

July 1951

I have always loved small towns. I love the warmth of friendship that comes when people meet casually for unhurried talk. There is an atmosphere of calm and a feeling that a man can stretch.

From the moment I graduated from the School of Pharmacy at the University of Nebraska in 1931, my wife, Dorothy, and I knew we wanted to buy a store in a small town. We discovered and fell in love with Wall, South Dakota, which was on the very border of the Badlands and then had a population of four hundred.

We bought a little drugstore on a shoestring. I was twenty-eight, my wife twenty-four, and the first of four children had arrived. Then came the Depression.

Even without a depression, many friends warned how hard it would be to succeed in a town of only four hundred people. Perhaps the town was small, with its one main street and hand-crank telephones, but it did have tourists motoring through to the Black Hills and points west.

At the start, business just trickled in: a rancher coming to town, a mother needing cough syrup, a tourist thirsty for a soda, or youngsters looking for penny candy. We barely hung on, living in the room behind the store. We couldn't afford adequate help, so Dorothy and I would switch back and forth from preparing baby bottles to dispensing sodas and pills.

Before settling in Wall, Dorothy and I had decided that the town of our choice should have a doctor, a bank, and most important, a church of our faith.

It was Father Connolly, our priest, who helped us so much during the Depression. He told us when we had first visited him: "You will make no mistake settling in Wall." Then in the difficult months that followed, his sermons constantly hammered: "You must persevere . . . persevere to the end."

We believe in praying first for what we want, then working to help make it come true. If we don't receive what we pray for, we are willing to accept God's decision. Perhaps God didn't want us to succeed with our drugstore.

Then one day it occurred to us that we had been missing a chance to do something for the tourists that passed through Wall. We liked small towns because of the warmth of the people. Were we reflecting this hospitality to our customers?

Suddenly Dorothy said to me: "Why don't we advertise free ice water?"

We both laughed at first as if it were a huge joke. Then the more we thought about it, the more the idea struck us. Why not!

Here we were in the heart of a hot, dusty area. Of course the travelers must be thirsty.

"Free Ice Water, Wall Drugstore, Wall, South Dakota." This was the sign we posted along the approaching highways.

"Ted," my wife said, "I think this is God's answer."

I knew what she meant. It wasn't the ice water itself, but what it stood for—friendliness.

The response was instant and heartwarming. Customers often stopped out of curiosity. Their unspoken question was, *What's your angle?* We met them with a genuine welcome and didn't try to sell them anything. But the glass of ice water was always waiting.

I think it was the very simplicity of the idea that caused it to go over so well.

Soon it was necessary to hire extra help and expand the store. Yet we never forgot how much we owed God for our success and how important it was to keep him always in the center of our activities.

In employing new help we asked applicants to furnish, as a reference, the name of their pastor. We encouraged our employees to go to church. Last summer one of our boys played the organ at the Lutheran church. Our own daughter played the organ at an early Mass.

Today our "free ice water" signs are as far away as Albany, New York. Some are even in Europe and Greenland. Many who stop say they drove miles out of their way just to see us. Last summer our twenty-eight employees dispensed an average of five thousand glasses of water a day. We also fill many prescriptions daily and serve gallons of ice cream, with everybody having a good time, including the Husteads.

What little success we have had, we owe to a couple of good strong backs, staying true to our work, and asking God for his help in the running of our business and our lives.

Believe, Believe, Believe

HARRY DeCAMP

May 1980

I am a man who lives today in a state of amazement. For sixty-six of my sixty-nine years, I had only a nodding relationship with God; how extraordinary, then, that when I was dying he would bother to reach down and heal me. And yet he did just that.

Even when I was told I had cancer of the bladder four years ago, my first thought was not that I should pray to God. In fact, I wasn't all that desperate; it didn't seem like the end of the world to me. Actually, it was harder on my wife Bess. Her mother had been a nurse, and Bess had been brought up hearing all the cancer horror stories. But I felt that somehow medicine was going to save me. I had confidence in my doctor, and I followed his instructions.

I eased up. I sold my insurance business to my son-in-law. Although I was in and out of the hospital several times, the cancer moved slowly. Life seemed fairly normal until February 1978, when I went to the hospital for exploratory surgery. When I returned from the recovery room, my doctor was there. "Harry," he said, "I consider myself a competent surgeon, but you need somebody much better than I am."

For the first time I was afraid.

But the doctor went on to say, "We're sending you to the Sloan-Kettering Cancer Center in New York. It's the best in the world." The idea that one of the finest surgeons in the world was going to operate on me gave me hope.

I knew when I went to New York that my bladder would have to be removed. As terrible as it was, I was prepared to live with the inconvenience of all kinds of medical contraptions. I was ready for anything if only I could be rid of the cancer.

But back from the recovery room on the day of the operation, through a haze of pain, I learned the truth. The great surgeon had sewn me up without removing my bladder. I cried in great racking sobs: My cancer was inoperable!

That afternoon, one of the surgeon's assistants came to talk to me.

"No lies," I said.

"Well . . ." he said, his brow furrowed with concentration, "the cancer has spread so extensively to the surrounding tissue that to remove it all would mean . . ." he trailed off lamely.

"How much time do I have?" I whispered.

"We can't promise you anything: a year, a month . . . or even a day."

I swallowed and licked my parched lips. "Where do I go from here?"

"I don't know," he replied.

Now I was facing the reality I hadn't faced before. I was going to die. They gave me some painkillers as big as thumbnails, and a supply of sleeping pills.

Bess, bless her, put on a brave show. "Now, Harry, we'll beat it yet," she said, as she propped me up in my easy chair in our living room. "We'll try the chemotherapy. And there are all sorts of other experimental treatments. . . ."

Somebody sent us literature from California about cancer patients being injected with massive doses of vitamin C. Bess pounced on it as if someone had thrown us a life preserver.

But I knew I was dying. Whenever I lay down, I felt as though I were smothering, so most of the time I sat in my easy chair and stared at meaningless images on the TV screen. I wondered if I could commit suicide, and if I did, what would be the best way?

The smell of food made me ill. "Harry!" Bess fumed. "I don't care if you're not hungry! EAT!"

I waved her away. What was the use? I'm a big man, but my weight plummeted steadily.

Occasionally I thought about praying to God, but I really didn't know how. I knew God was there, but he was some mystical being, far away. It didn't seem right that after I'd ignored him all these years, I should start begging now. The words I said seemed to bounce off the ceiling.

Then two things happened, one right after the other.

The first was the card. It didn't seem to be that much different from all the other get-well cards. Yet for some reason, I kept returning to it. A friend had scribbled a message beneath her name: "With God all things are possible" (Matthew 19:26).

How I wanted that to be true! Again and again I'd take out the card and look at it. *Suppose it were true . . . how do you go about making contact with God? Isn't it too late in the game to think about going to church? Should I pray harder? Read the Bible?* I floundered; I was so confused I didn't know what to do. Yet the phrase kept coming back to me, "all things are possible."

Then the magazine came—an issue of *Guideposts*—with a cover story about a cancer victim. She too was sent home to die—just like me. But she refused to die. Instead she began to read and reread the healings of Jesus in the New Testament. She prayed constantly. She went to God determined that he was going to heal her. "Most of the time," she said, "we knock on the door so timidly and open it just a little crack. We really don't expect God to reply."

Wasn't that what I was doing? Wasn't I knocking timidly? Should I knock more boldly, like the woman in that story?

In the same issue of that magazine, there was the story about a seriously wounded soldier who recovered by creating mental pictures of himself as a healthy, whole individual. The soldier also went to Jesus with utter confidence. He trusted the words of Jesus Christ that "whatever you ask in prayer, believe that you have received it, and it will be yours" (Mark 11:24, RSV).

For the next three days, I spent all my waking hours reading and rereading those two articles. I read them a dozen times—three dozen times. I saturated my consciousness until the details of what these two people had done became part of me. The thing that both of them had in common was a simple, childlike trust that God loved them and would heal them. I decided that I was going to believe the same way they did. Right there in our living room, while Bess was clattering about in the kitchen and the TV was blaring with the noise of a game show, I bowed my head.

"God," I said with conviction. "I am knocking on the door. I am here before you to say that I know without any doubt in the world that you are going to heal me."

Don't ask me to explain, but in that one incredible moment, the door swung open. For the first time in my life, God was close to me. He was at my elbow. He was there. And for the first time in prayer, I felt as if I was talking to Somebody, not just to myself. A deep joy stirred within me.

"Bess! Bess!" I called out. Bess came running. I wanted to tell her what had happened, but I didn't have the words yet.

"Yes, Harry? What's the matter?"

"I'm hungry," I said.

She looked at me peculiarly. "Would you like a cup of tea?"

"No." I said, "I want food." At first she thought I was kidding. I hadn't asked for anything in over four weeks. So she kidded back. "Well, why don't I run out and get you a nice big submarine sandwich?"

"Fine," I said with a grin.

And Bess did just that. She ran out and bought a sandwich of ham, cheese, tomato, and lettuce, and she watched in astonishment as I ate every bit of it with gusto. She was only a bit less surprised when I ate a full breakfast the next morning, after my first full night's sleep in bed in weeks, and then took a walk—just a short one.

For the first two days after I found God, I prayed, not in the old, stilted, self-conscious, unbelieving way, but in my new informal faith way. I prayed as I walked, I prayed while I sat in my easy chair, and I prayed when I went to bed. I was having a nonstop conversation with God, in whom I now believed and trusted with all my heart.

On the third day, like the soldier in the story, I began to picture my healing with images just as clear as if they were coming in on our TV screen. I could see an army of white blood cells, led by Jesus Christ, sweeping down from my shoulders into my stomach, swirling around in my bladder, battling their way into my liver and my heart. Regiment after regiment, they advanced, the white corpuscles moving relentlessly on the cancer cells, moving in and devouring them! On and on the victorious white army swept, down into my legs and feet and toes, then to the top of my body, mopping up stray cancer cells as they went, until, at last, the battle was over and Jesus Christ stood in triumph.

Day after day I replayed that battle scene in my mind. It made me feel terrific. I felt full of health. My energy returned dramatically. I walked, drove my car, played eighteen holes of golf and walked all the way. I dutifully went through with my chemotherapy treatments, but more to please Bess and my doctor than myself.

Six months later, I went back to my original doctor for an examination. He seemed surprised to see me looking so healthy and well.

I tried to prepare him. "Look, Doc," I said, "you're not going to find a thing. Believe me. I'm all better!"

Smiling indulgently he replied, "Well, Harry, let's take a look anyway, shall we?"

He performed several tests and found that the malignant mass behind the bladder had disappeared. Everything seemed to be normal. The doctor was astounded but, nevertheless, cautious.

"Harry," he said, "the only way we can prove conclusively that you're free of cancer is to do another exploratory. But you look so healthy that we're not about to do that. We'll keep an eye on you, but it looks very good."

That was over a year ago, and today I feel fit as a fiddle. So I continue to live in a state of amazement. I'm amazed at God's love. I'm amazed at his closeness. I'm amazed that it's all so simple, though I've spent my life making it so complicated. Jesus told us the way to be healed—simply, powerfully, in two words, " . . . only believe."

Joey's Trial

BONNIE LA MOUNTAIN

March 1990

My husband and I had just popped a bowl of popcorn and slipped a movie into the VCR on that clear spring night three years ago, the kind of night when fear and worry seem as far away as the stars. We were ready to settle in for a cozy evening in our home outside Sacramento. As the opening credits blinked on the screen, the ring of the phone shattered our peace. "Wouldn't you know?" I muttered, springing up from the couch to answer as Brad punched the pause button on the remote control.

"There's been an accident," said the caller. "Your son has run over a man. You'd better get down here."

Joey? In an accident? It was the call every parent dreads. We jumped in the car and sped to the scene just a few blocks away, right across from our church. We were tense and silent as Brad parked near a swelling throng of onlookers who were illuminated by the piercing strobes of several police cruisers. We saw Joey's Ford in the middle of the street. And there on the pavement lay the sprawled figure of an elderly man, with paramedics working over him.

Brad spotted Joey, and we threaded through the crowd to his side. Thank God he was safe. Our eighteen-year-old was ashen-faced as a police lieutenant interrogated him. Joey saw us and broke down. "I didn't see him!" he cried. "Suddenly he was just there, out of nowhere. Is he going to be all right?"

All I could do was hold Joey tightly and tell him not to be afraid. From the crowd I heard a voice say, "Kid must have been drunk."

"That's not true!" I shot back. Joey was a good son.

Brad put his arm around me as the policeman warned Joey not to speak to us until he was through being questioned. Other officers took statements from witnesses and checked Joey's car, testing the lights and brakes. As the ambulance sped away with a howl, the lieutenant called us aside. "You and Joey can go home now," he said. "We'll let you know about the report."

Early next morning the phone rang. It was the police. "I'm sorry," said the officer, "the man your son hit died."

I thought about the man's family and said a silent prayer. I dreaded breaking the news to Joey. He'd be devastated. When Joey came down for breakfast, his hopeful blue eyes ringed and puffy, I knew he hadn't slept. There'd be no easy way to tell him.

"He died this morning, Son,"

Joey pushed away his plate. "Did he have anyone?" he asked softly.

"Yes," I replied, barely able to return Joey's anguished gaze, "he had a family."

The next few days were somber ones around our house. Joey seemed lost in his own world of pain and guilt. We sent a wreath to the family, knowing that it couldn't begin to express the sadness we felt. Anonymously I slipped into the back of the church for the funeral.

A few days later the police absolved Joey of any wrongdoing. The investigating officers concluded that the pedestrian had carelessly stepped into the poorly lit street from between parked cars. With the report finally released and Joey cleared, we were ready to get on with our lives.

A few days later a stranger knocked at our door. "Joey home?" he snapped. Something about the man's surly tone and rumpled appearance frightened me. I didn't like the way he looked me up and down and tried to peek into the house. I informed him Joey was out.

"Where can I find him?" he demanded, whipping out a notepad.

"He's with his girlfriend," I answered, immediately sorry that I'd surrendered the information. I asked who he was. He claimed to be a private detective but refused to show any identification or discuss his business. "You'll be seeing me again," he growled.

The visit left me shaken. I thought the investigation was over and done with. A day or so later, however, we found our ordeal just beginning. Another stranger appeared at the door, this time with a sheaf of legal documents. Joey had been named in a one-million-dollar wrongful-death suit brought by the widow.

"What are we going to do?" I asked Brad as Joey looked on anxiously.

"We've got nothing to worry about," Brad insisted. "The police have already cleared Joey." Nevertheless, we decided to see a lawyer.

What we learned shocked us. The police report carried virtually no weight in a civil proceeding. It merely exculpated Joey of any criminal wrongdoing. In a civil suit Joey would have to clear his name all over again. Moreover, opined the lawyer, most juries are prejudiced against teenage drivers.

"But how can I be sued if I didn't do anything wrong?" Joey wanted to know. I didn't have an answer.

The phone rang as we were talking. It was the private detective. He insisted on speaking with Joey.

"I'm sorry," I told him. "We've been advised not to discuss this case."

"What I want to know," he snarled, "is what you good people have to hide." Then he hung up.

Cold fear shot through me. This was like a nightmare. How were we going to defend ourselves? We knew our son was innocent, but could we convince a jury? The lawyer had painted a bleak picture. If Joey was found even partly responsible for the death, he could be hounded for years and forced to surrender his earnings, his possessions, his future. He would be destroyed.

Our life became a frustrating tangle of legal red tape. At first I wanted to hire the best lawyers money could buy. We'd sell the house if we had to. Anything to protect Joey. But Brad prevailed on me to try it his way. The lawyer offered to guide Joey through the preliminary steps of defending himself, saving on legal fees. Our hope was the case would never reach trial.

The law was an intimidating morass of torts, depositions, and motions. My waking hours were increasingly devoted to worrying about Joey and the case. My nights grew short and sleepless, and when I did sleep I always awoke to a sense of foreboding. I suffered chronic headaches, nausea, and nervousness. I doted on Joey and spent less time with my two other children, Eric, ten, and Kim, eight. Sometimes I'd sit and dream about how serene and tidy our life was before the accident, what a beautiful baby Joey had been and how I wished this had never happened.

One day the detective returned. I again refused to give him any information. "Look, lady," he shouted at me, his face flushing crimson, "you and that kid have to talk! Sooner or later, I'll get you!"

"Get out of here!" I screamed back. "Get off our property! Joey didn't do anything wrong! Leave us alone!"

Eventually we had to get a restraining order from the court to keep him away.

The months of uncertainty took their toll on Joey. He grew withdrawn and silent. His once-ready smile vanished. He began missing time at his construction job. Our pastor suggested counseling, and Joey agreed. I was relieved that there was someplace for Joey to go to get his feelings out. But I was haunted by the fact that perhaps I was setting a poor example for him. He knew how scared I was. Was he afraid to talk out his feelings at home because he didn't think I could handle it?

One day I received a letter from my mom. "Bonnie, remember when you were a little girl and would wake up crying from a nightmare?" she wrote. "I'd come in to you, and you always felt better after repeating something I'd taught you to say: 'Be not afraid, for God is watching over me.' I think it's time for you to start saying it again."

I remembered those nightmares. I was easily scared as a child. Mom's advice was so simple and elegant, so direct. But I had a grown-up nightmare. *Be not afraid . . .* would this be enough to overcome my fear now? I thumbed through an old prayer book trying to find a verse I vaguely remembered. Finally I came upon it in Mark 5:36, "Don't be afraid. Just trust Me" (The Living Bible).

I had stopped trusting God to see us through this mess. Fear had poured into the void my absent trust left behind the way water fills a ship's leaky hull. I said the words to myself: *Be not afraid, for God is watching over me.* I repeated them and began to feel soothed, reassured. I remembered how the accident had taken place within sight of our church, a reminder that God had been with us all along.

After Mom's letter, I used that little prayer whenever fear boiled up. When the phone rang or a subpoena appeared, I'd say it. *Be not afraid. . . .*

I think I set an example for Joey; he too began to get on with his life. I shared the prayer with him. We both used it when the going got tough. The day he was scheduled to give a pretrial deposition to the widow's attorney was one of our toughest. I was told I could stay in the room while Joey was questioned, provided I remained silent and composed.

The lawyer was ruthless with Joey, pushing him, cajoling him, and shouting trick questions. At first I could tell how nervous my son was. When he was little, Joey had a stuttering problem. Now he began to stammer again as the lawyer posed leading questions about that night, insinuating that Joey was dreaming about his girlfriend instead of watching the road. I wanted to jump out of my chair and answer the questions myself. Instead I said the words silently, *Be not afraid, for God is watching over us.*

Joey pulled through like a champ. After his initial hesitation he spoke clearly and told the truth. By the end of the long afternoon, we knew we were safe. And not too long after that, nearly two years from the accident, I got a phone call from our attorney.

"Bonnie," he said, "the widow has decided to drop the suit."

It was hard to believe—the nightmare had finally ended. But the end had really come much earlier when my mother reminded me about my girlhood prayer. That is when the fear was over.

Our life is back to normal. Joey married the girl he was visiting the night of the accident. She was by his side through the whole ordeal. I believe the widow's lawsuit was simply part of the agonizing grieving process she was going through, something purgative she felt she had to do. I can't let myself feel any bitterness over it. She suffered a tremendous loss, and it is not for me to judge.

Besides, in the process I found something I had left behind long ago—my little prayer of faith that reassured me I need not fear, for God is always watching. In the loving presence of God, there can be no fear.

"I'M NOT SUPPOSED TO give these away," the young man said, handing me a display Bible, "but I sense you should have this." I shrugged and absently tucked it away. We had a Bible at home. I'd only stopped by the Gideons table because nothing else at the Iowa State Fair was set up.

A few days later I was walking to town when a car pulled up beside me. "Get in," the driver snarled, pointing a gun at me.

I did as he said. Soon he pulled over, grabbed me, and tried to force me down on the seat. I struggled with all my strength. Finally he ordered me out of the car.

Before both my feet were on the ground, I heard a shot and felt a sharp pain in my side. I collapsed and the man came around the car. He picked up my purse, took out my wallet, then threw the purse on my head and shot it. I felt a dreadful impact. Still conscious, I lay silent, hoping he would think I was dead. I heard the car drive away, and I stumbled to a nearby farmhouse. A woman called for help, and the police and an ambulance arrived shortly. Even as I was being rushed to the hospital, the police were closing in on the drug-crazed driver based on the description I'd given them.

At the hospital, just before I went into surgery to remove the bullet in my side, my sister came to see me. "Do you know what saved your life, Mavis?" she asked.

She handed me the Bible that had been in my purse. A bullet was lodged in it, its tip stopping exactly at Psalm 37:14–15: "The wicked draw the sword, and bend the bow . . . to slay those whose ways are upright. But their swords will pierce their own hearts, and their bows will be broken."

—MAVIS GUSTAFSON PIGFORD, *November 1999*

What Angie Taught Me

DARCIE HARRIS

April 1997

We moved back to Oklahoma City on Memorial Day weekend in 1982. I was delighted to be among old friends again. Most of all, I was happy our children, four-year-old Angie and three-year-old Tate, would grow up in the place I called home. *Life is good,* I thought as we drove up to our house in historic Mesta Park.

Just a few weeks later, my world was shattered. A pediatric neurologist diagnosed Angie with a brain tumor. "I'm sorry," he said. "It's inoperable. I'm afraid there's not much we can do."

Almost by reflex I prayed, *God, please make Angie well.*

Now, on a warm summer night, I tucked Angie in bed, stroking her soft blond hair. "What would you like me to read?" I asked.

"The bunny book, Mommy," she said.

It was one of our favorites. But this time I had trouble concentrating on the words I read because I kept thinking about all the things Angie would never experience. She would miss so much. I could picture her in nervous anticipation on the first day of kindergarten. I could see her big brown eyes glowing as her date awkwardly pinned a corsage on her dress before her prom. I could hear her laughter as I taught her how to drive. I could imagine her in cap and gown, walking down the aisle at high school graduation.

I still hardly believed it was my little girl the neurologist had been talking about. Angie, who had never had more than a minor ear infection since the day she was born. She hadn't been her usual buoyant self lately, but I had chalked it up to our move. Her balance and coordination seemed off. I had assumed it was an awkward growth spurt. The doctor visit had been a precaution, but I had never expected . . .

I begged God to do something. I wanted to believe he could heal my daughter—that he had the power to make the tumor go away. But deep inside, true faith was hard to find.

Why Angie?

Angie was pure—pure sweetness, pure goodness, pure innocence, pure love. Her disarming smile penetrated even the most cynical walls of adults. If this could happen to her, nothing made sense anymore. Nothing felt safe or sure—not even God.

As Angie drifted off to sleep, I closed the storybook and kissed her forehead. *I followed all the rules*, I thought. I had used car seats from the day each baby came home from the hospital. I had dressed them in flame-retardant pajamas, and put safety plugs in all the electrical outlets. *How could this happen after I've been so careful? Tell me, God. How?* I thought I had been such a good mother.

In July, Angie underwent radiation therapy. Much braver

than I, she took the daily hospital visits without complaint. I kept praying for a miracle.

The radiation therapy brought some results. One day shortly after she finished the six-week course of treatment, I asked her, "Would you like to go shopping with me?"

Excited at the prospect of one of her favorite activities, she squealed, "Just girls, no boys!" It was her way of letting me know she wanted my undivided attention.

"Of course," I said, laughing. I turned and bent down to hug her.

She giggled and hugged me back. I wanted never to let go of her.

The next four months we lived as close to normal as we could. Angie rode her tricycle up and down the sidewalk with her little brother, Tate, and outfitted her dolls in elaborate costumes. She seemed so much like herself again that at times I cautiously allowed myself to wonder if a miracle had happened after all. I was afraid to ask God if it could be true.

But on Christmas Day, as I watched Angie open her presents, I noticed the dreaded signs—an uneven gait, a slightly crooked smile. The tumor was growing again.

My dim hopes were extinguished. Fear and then anger took over. *God, how can you abandon us?* I demanded. So many prayers—from me, from our family and friends, even from strangers who had heard about Angie's illness—and all of them unanswered. What use was it to turn to God?

Angie began experimental chemotherapy in January, a last-resort treatment.

Balloons, gifts, games, and friends filled the house as we celebrated her fifth birthday, knowing it would probably be her last.
The day after, Angie and I sat down with a box of note cards.
"We're going to send cards to your friends who came to your birthday party," I explained. "On the front of the cards, it says, 'Thank
you.' What would you like me to write on the inside?"

Eyes sparkling, she answered without hesitation, "For all
the love."

A month of chemotherapy did nothing to slow the growth of
the tumor. Angie's speech became slurred, and she was losing
mobility in her right side. When I asked the neurologist what to
expect, he told me as gently as he could that Angie would gradually lose the use of her limbs and the ability to speak and swallow.

As her condition deteriorated, Angie was content to spend
time with me on the living room sofa, reading, dressing her dolls,
and filling a scrapbook with stickers. She loved playing with
makeup and earrings, and looked forward to visits from friends.
Really, Angie adjusted to her limitations better than I did.

She never complained about having to spend her days in the
house instead of being out playing in the snow, but I felt enough
frustration for both of us.

With help from friends and family, I was able to take care of
Angie's everyday needs. But the responsibility of helping her
understand what was going to happen weighed on me. Her doctor referred me to a child psychiatrist, who told me what Angie
needed was the truth—honest information coupled with love and
reassurance. It was time to talk about death.

How could I help her accept the fact that she was going to

die when it was impossible for me to accept it?

My faith might have wavered, but I had always believed without question that in heaven Angie would be healed, whole, safe. In my desperation I clung to that thin thread of belief and made one more appeal to God. *I can't do this alone,* I prayed. *Please, I need your help.*

That night, I tucked the covers around Angie's chin and gently touched her cheek. She piped up. "Mommy, can you read *The Runaway Bunny*?"

"Of course," I said. I picked up the book and launched into the familiar story. A spirited bunny tells his mother he's going to run away, and she says she will run after him. Then he says he will become a fish in a stream. Mama bunny replies that she will become a fisherman and find him.

So the story goes . . . if he becomes a bird, she will be the tree that he flies home to; if he turns into a sailboat, she will become the wind. Each time the bunny imagines a different guise, his mother steadfastly assures him that wherever he is, she will be with him.

Then Angie interrupted. "Mommy, when I die," she asked, "will you die too?"

I felt my heart break.

Taking her hand in mine, I struggled to stay calm. "A part of me will die when you die, Angie," I answered carefully. "The part of me that you need will go with you, wherever you go."

She gave me a questioning look.

"You know, the same as in the story," I said. "No matter where the bunny went, his mama followed him."

I squeezed Angie's hand a little tighter. Her speech was

impaired, and within a few days she would no longer be able to walk. But that night she spoke about her death with more courage than the bravest of men could display.

I knew finally where God was. He was with Angie, giving her strength and courage and hope; and he was also with me, giving me the words my daughter needed to hear.

When she asked me about heaven, I told her I believed there she would walk, dance, and play again. She snuggled close. "If I have to die," she said, "I want you holding me, and my family around me."

One month later that's how it happened. It was hard, but faith made my grief easier to bear. In time I came to understand that God had done for me exactly what the mama bunny did for her runaway.

God hadn't abandoned me. He had been with me—every step of the way. And he would always be there for me. Just as the love Angie and I shared would never fade, neither would God's love.

I am not going to pretend that I don't miss my daughter every single day. Or that in the years since her death I have learned to handle all problems gracefully. I have good days and bad, but far more good.

There have been occasions I felt bereft and alone, just as I did when she was sick. I have questioned God because he didn't immediately answer my prayers.

At times like those, I think about what Angie taught me: *God is here, right here with me.*

Then I picture my daughter, happy and healthy in heaven. I remember her words on her final birthday, and I say a grateful prayer, "Thank you, God, for all the love."

Closer to Him

Elizabeth Sherrill

June 2000

By age twenty-two, I'd experienced various kinds of pain—everything from family bereavement to root canal surgery without anesthetics. But there was one kind of suffering I'd never imagined . . . the pain of feeling betrayed by God.

If I thought of God at all, it was only to dismiss his existence. Then, in Fleetwood, New York, where my husband, John, and I had settled into our first apartment, I came across this type of suffering for the first time. Though it's been more than fifty years since we lived next door to Henry and Martha, I can still hear Henry's anguished question, "What did Martha ever do that God should punish her so?"

Martha—only three years older than I at the time—was dying of cancer of the spine. Henry didn't need to describe her agony. The apartment walls were thin. His wife's pain, though so much worse than anything I'd experienced, was at least something I could relate to. Henry's was not. The idea of pain as punishment had never even occurred to me.

On the contrary, I'd learned from a college roommate at Northwestern the important function pain served in daily life. Lucinda's mother had an illness that rendered her unable to feel pain. She couldn't tell when water scalded or when she stepped on something sharp. She needed a human guardian to do the work that pain does for the rest of us.

But pain served no protecting purpose in our next-door neighbor's situation. Martha suffered a brutal, unceasing torture. Henry's response was to rage at God.

Unbearable though my own painful episodes had seemed as I was going through them, I hadn't held God responsible. You can't be angry at someone you don't believe in. But Henry and Martha were deeply religious. "She never missed a Sunday at church!" was one of Henry's most bitter cries.

When, some years later, I took my own first tentative steps in faith, the memory of Henry's torment was the chief obstacle I wrestled with. If I were to believe in an all-good, all-powerful God, I too would have to confront the why of such suffering as Martha's. Pain would become not only a physical and emotional ordeal, but a spiritual one.

Searching for answers, John and I began attending various churches to find some of the ways believers deal with the dilemma of suffering.

In one place we were told that pain was only an illusion of the mind. When I had to take our two-year-old daughter, Liz, who had an excruciating earache, out of the service, we were followed to the church parking lot by several members of the congregation. They told us reproachfully that the cause of her suffering was not an infection, but my belief that the ache was real.

We met others who saw pain as a wake-up call. Several years after we left the Fleetwood apartment, John underwent cancer surgery. He was visited in the hospital by the pastor of a church we'd attended a few months previously. The postoperative pain John was feeling was a foretaste—a mild foretaste, the man stressed—of the pains of hell awaiting those who have turned their backs on God.

Still others saw pain as a teaching device. "I think God was telling you not to climb so high," a technician told our eight-year-old son, Scott, as she X-rayed his broken arm.

Pain as punishment, pain as a creation of the mind, pain as warning, pain as schoolmaster—I could find some sense in all these interpretations. A stomachache will punish me for an eating binge. My mental attitude does affect how much something hurts. A chest pain may remind me of my mortality. And every experience teaches.

But none of these explanations completely satisfied me. Pain often has nothing to do with what I've eaten or anything else I do. Animals don't "believe" in pain, but they surely experience it. Pain may drive some people, who otherwise would not, to seek God, but it also afflicts the devout. And it often teaches us what we know only too well.

Pain played a role in my own commitment to Jesus. An experience of John's moved our search for God out of the realm of the theoretical.

During a second cancer surgery in 1959, John's lungs collapsed while he was on the operating table and a four-hour battle for his life was waged over his unconscious form. All that John knew, waking in the recovery room, was that a cat's cradle of tubes protruded from his chest and that he was in the most intense pain of his life. The pain was not only physical but emotional, as he assumed the cancer, which in fact had been contained, must have metastasized throughout his chest.

Into that pain-filled place came Jesus. He came as light, "light, impossibly bright," John told me later, "light that was a being." In that radiant presence, John's first thought, to his own amazement, was to pray for others in the recovery room whose moans he'd been hearing. Immediately, the moans ceased.

John's own pain did not. Hadn't he asked Jesus, I wanted to know, to take away the pain? But he had not. He had encountered something infinitely more compelling than pain, and in the joy and wonder of that meeting, pain had ceased to be his focus.

It was the beginning of a relationship with God for both of us. Stunned by John's experience, I began to read the Bible and discovered that the mystery of suffering has occupied far wiser minds than mine ever since Adam and Eve were driven from the garden.

In the Bible's sixty-six books, I came across many portrayals of God's role in pain. I found the God of wrath, whose lightning bolts may be averted with gifts. I met the righteous Judge, who sends just punishment on a guilty people. But I also saw the compassionate God, in both the Old and New Testaments, who heals his people's pain rather than causes it.

One of the most famous examinations of the issue is in the Book of Job. Written centuries before the birth of Christ, the story asks, as did our neighbor Henry: Why do the righteous suffer? Pious, prayerful Job had been assaulted by overwhelming physical and emotional agony. His friends insisted that such pain must be punishment for some secret sin. Or perhaps a warning against pride.

Although Job never resolves the why of pain, he rejects these simplistic answers, maintaining his faith in a God of love. So do the scores of faithful people I've met in writing for *Guideposts* for over half a century—people with lives and bodies ravaged by war, accident, illness, but with spirits that radiate joy.

All attest that suffering has brought them closer to God. I too find as time goes by—right now in the arthritis that makes me shift as I write—that the why of pain becomes less important than something else. Or someone else.

The figure of Jesus on the cross has become, for me, the answer to the question Henry first made me consider: How can I believe in a loving God in a hurting world? I like to think that in time Henry's faith showed him the same answer. When I look at the cross, I don't see a remote and righteous God, using pain to reform a sinful world. Nor do I see a disembodied spirit, dismissing the physical world as unimportant. I see Jesus naked, bleeding and gasping, bearing not only terrible physical pain, but the anguish of bringing sorrow to those who loved him and the spiritual desolation of separation from God.

What kind of pain could ever come to me that Jesus does not know? A nine-year-old boy, named Darrell, said it best. I heard his words from Erva Merow, a hospital volunteer in Kenosha, Wisconsin.

All Erva could see of little Darrell Truax were his lips and one blistered cheek; the rest of his body was wrapped in layer upon layer of sterile gauze. The fire that had burned him so terribly had taken the lives of four of his family members.

The magnitude of his suffering kept most visitors away from Darrell's room. Even Erva had to escape when the nurses came to turn him. From far down the corridor, she could hear his screams as his seared flesh was touched. One day another patient called out to her: "How can God do this to an innocent child?"

"Don't say anything against God!" Erva heard Darrell's voice ring out. "When it hurts, God cries with me."

Fear No Evil

NORMA WALLACE

March 2002

*I*t's strange, looking back on that day, Tuesday, October 9, how I can pinpoint the exact moment it happened.

It was an otherwise perfectly ordinary day as I sorted mail at the Trenton Processing and Distribution Center in Hamilton, New Jersey. My supervisor assigned me to machine number 11. Number 11 is an automated behemoth the size of an eighteen-wheeler tractor-trailer truck, with the capacity to handle thousands of letters per minute. As I fed mail into the machine, a computerized scanner read the address on each piece of mail, sorted it by zip code, and applied a bar code on the back indicating its destination, right down to the carrier route, all in the blink of an electronic eye.

Not too long into my shift, Number 11 jammed. I checked the feeder and the modules, then called my supervisor, who sent over a mechanic. "I can't find anything either, Norma," he said. Given the volume of mail we handle, jams on these machines happen from time to time. I knew it was probably a single piece of mail wedged in somewhere, so I opened up the feeder module. Finally I found the culprit, a bulky envelope. I reached in and pulled it free. "I got it!"

Number 11 started up again, a river of mail flowing by in a blur. Seeing the mail move like that always gave me a sense of satisfaction, knowing that I was a part of the vital system of communication our country depends on. We all count on the mail getting through, from bills to birthday cards. Even we postal workers get that little jolt of anticipation when we check our mailboxes each day.

Suddenly Number 11 shut down once more. This time it was a computer malfunction. A technician took a look and confirmed that some kind of dust was blocking the electronic scanning eye.

He took an air gun and blew out the dust. I stepped aside and turned away, not wanting to breathe anything in. In September, letters to NBC News and the *New York Post* containing a potent form of powdered anthrax had been postmarked at our facility. Like the rest of the nation, we could only wonder who was behind such an inconceivably evil act. Almost as inconceivable to me was the chance that that same evil could somehow reach right into my own life, into my own body. Certainly I was concerned. Everyone was. I just couldn't imagine it happening to me.

Not that my life hadn't had its share of challenges. As a single mother for the past twenty-five years, I had worked hard at supporting and raising my two kids, Ramona Lisa and Coleman Wesley. I named my son after my brother, the Reverend Coleman Wallace. Doctors found a tumor in my womb when I was pregnant with my son. Neither one of us was given more than a fifty percent chance of surviving. That's where my faith came in. My grandfather taught me to read using the Bible as my primer. During that difficult pregnancy, my brother and the rest of my family helped me lean on the faith I'd been raised with, and my faith not only sustained me but grew and deepened, so that when little Coleman and I both came through our ordeal just fine, I knew that with the Lord at my side I need never fear any evil.

That weekend after my shift on Number 11, I felt sick to my stomach. Monday night I started running a fever, and on Tuesday I struggled into work. The plant manager called everyone into the conference room and alerted us to the threat of deadly anthrax bacteria. By the time I punched out, I was shaking with chills one minute and sweating profusely the next. *This is bad,* I thought, and called my doctor.

Dr. Berna wasn't in, but her partner saw me right away. He began treating me for a viral syndrome.

I went home and crawled into bed, sicker than I had ever been in my life, even during my pregnancy with Coleman. Though my mind recoiled in dread at the thought, I found myself wondering, *Could I have anthrax? Lord, I don't want to leave this earth because of some bug or bacteria.* At once I felt an intense light fill my inner being.

Still I worsened by the day. On Friday my temperature soared above 102 degrees. Alarmed, Dr. Berna sent me to the emergency room at Virtua Memorial Hospital, where a pulmonary specialist and the head of infectious diseases, suspecting severe pneumonia, admitted me.

For the next forty-eight hours, I was so ill that I barely knew what was happening. I do remember the pain when they aspirated the fluid that was drowning my lungs by inserting two tubes into my chest. I remember watching the ceiling rush by as I was rolled from X-ray to CAT scan, an IV pumping antibiotics into my veins trailing behind. And I remember how I knew for sure I had anthrax. I awoke my third morning in the hospital to see a doctor from the Centers for Disease Control standing at my bedside. She wasn't there just because I had pneumonia.

By then the antibiotics seemed to be helping me hold my own, but just barely. I still felt like a fire was burning in my lungs and consuming all the oxygen.

Once again my brother was there, holding my hand tight while he prayed. "The whole congregation is with you right now, Norma," he said. "They are holding you up in prayer." I could feel the strength of their prayers as surely as I felt the antibiotics coursing into my arm.

Then the news broke that two postal workers from a sorting facility like mine in Washington, D.C., had died of inhalation anthrax. My mind jumped back two weeks to my shift on Number 11. I remembered my hand reaching in to clear out the bulky envelope that had jammed the machine. I saw the technician blow the dust off the electronic eye. I'd read a report about how the anthrax bacteria invades the body. "According to this report, I'm going to die," I told my daughter, Ramona Lisa, who was sitting at my bedside. "But I'm ready."

"What will you believe? That report? I believe in Jesus Christ. No, Mother, you're going to live!"

At that she clutched my hand and began praying out loud. *Fear no evil,* I thought, *fear no evil for the Lord is with me. No evil can defeat you, hallelujah!*

I clung to that promise as anthrax ravaged me. Every time I opened my eyes, someone was in the room praying: my son, my daughter, my brother, and other relatives and friends, as well as a whole host of angels—doctors, nurses, and custodians. Even the security guards tiptoed into my room to pray for me. And always, that healing inner light of the Holy Spirit gave me the strength to battle on, breath by breath. *The Lord is with me. . . .*

Even before Dr. Trudo, my pulmonologist, listened to my breathing on the tenth day and told me I had turned the corner, I knew I was getting better. "It must be God, Norma," he said, "because they sure didn't teach us about anthrax in medical school."

On November 5, my son took me home. It wasn't until then, when I faced all the questions from the news media, that I realized how my illness was part of a larger fight this country was waging against terrorism.

Terrorism is an evil that preys on the innocent. Even when bioterrorism does not affect us directly, it sickens us with fear and dread and saps the strength of our spirits. Yet I have known the strength that the Lord avails us in these times. No evil can prevail when he is with us.

Unexpected Blessings

Who Wove the Robe?

Dorothea M. Hulse

April 1955

W e want an absolutely seamless robe, as exact as you can make it in texture, color, and weave to the one Christ wore."

This was my assignment from Charles Le Maire, wardrobe director at Twentieth Century Fox, some six months before the studio was to begin filming *The Robe*, based on the famous novel by the late Lloyd C. Douglas.

Weaving this robe was to be the biggest adventure of my life . . . an adventure climaxed by near calamity.

First came four months of intensive research as Mr. Le Maire and I combed every yarn house in this country and Europe before we found the exact grade of sheep's wool yarn. Then, more weeks of making samples for texture and color. We spent days brewing dyes of walnut hulls, such as were used in Galilee two thousand years ago.

So immersed did my family and I become in the life and

times of Jesus and in the miracles of his power that we were only mildly surprised when "coincidences" nudged our work along.

First our research was suddenly simplified when at home I came across a rare book "The Dictionary of the Bible" by James Hastings, published in 1909. Left to me by my father, the Reverend Willard Aldrich, it contained descriptions of how yarn was spun, dyed, and woven in Galilee in the first century.

Next, Eddie Azzam, a young pupil in my Sunday school class at the Los Angeles First Methodist Church, happened to mention that he had lived in Palestine. The lad proved it by bringing me a seamless robe from Bethlehem, where it was sold as a copy of the robe actually worn by Christ.

Because the walnut dye photographed a lifeless brown, we decided to add henna to it. Later, by chance, we discovered that a French monastery had a fragment believed to be from Christ's robe itself, and that it had the same reddish color.

When my daughter, Dorothy Lou Macready, and I finally started to weave the robe, our thoughts and words focused on the man who wore the original. We discussed the woman whose son Jesus healed. It was this mother's gratitude, according to one tradition, that prompted her to weave the robe. An arduous task, this style of weaving was originally done in certain sections of Egypt—and during the Master's lifetime only in the province of Galilee.

We recalled the scene at the foot of the cross, where soldiers cast lots for the robe—how its symbolism had lived nearly two thousand years.

These quiet weekends of work on the loom contained many golden moments as we relived the story of Jesus.

At 4:30 one Sunday afternoon—the day before production was to begin on *The Robe*—Dorothy Lou and I wove the final thread. My small grandson drew close, small hands reaching out to touch.

It was finished. The next morning at nine, it would be at the studio. We counted up the months of research and the hours of actual weaving—three hours for each five inches—thirty-six hours in all, not counting warping the loom.

At that moment a look of anguish froze my daughter's face. I turned hastily to see my three-year-old grandson standing with a pair of shears in one hand and a large piece of the robe in the other. All our effort was gone in the twinkling of a bright pair of scissors!

Thousands of dollars in talent, sets, and stars, the maximum effort of a large studio scheduled to begin work at nine in the morning, exactly sixteen hours away . . . and the robe, a thirty-six-hour job—not counting the time to rewarp the loom—gouged beyond repair.

Oddly enough, the thought that thirty-six hours of weaving couldn't be done in sixteen hours didn't occur to me until much later. The first thought that came was, *pray*. The second was *work*.

As Dorothy Lou and I started a new robe, our fingers flying, I thought back to a certain childhood experience when I was eight . . . a picnic with my best girlfriend, Mary Oliver. Before leaving, I had talked my cross and disagreeable landlady into lending me a luggage strap for my bicycle.

When we were ready to start for home late that afternoon, we couldn't find the luggage strap. Up and down the banks of the stream, in and out of the apple orchard, we searched to no avail. At last, in tears, we did the only thing we knew. We knelt down and prayed, then arose and walked back into the orchard. Sure enough, there it lay in the grass. To my young mind, it seemed completely understandable.

Now here I was, a grown woman and a grandmother, sitting before my loom praying . . . and expecting results. For it is my belief that, "except ye remain as little children," or develop and renew that simple faith of a child, you miss the results that can happen through pure trust.

So my daughter and I prayed and worked through the night while her two children slept nearby, under some hand-woven shawls.

At exactly two o'clock in the morning, Dorothy Lou and I were once more weaving the final threads on the robe. In just nine hours we had rewarped and completed a job that had taken thirty-six hours before. Later, when we did two extra robes, each took thirty-six hours again, although there was no variation in technique or honest application and effort.

When Dorothy looked at the hands of the clock as we completed that second robe, she said in a very small voice, "Nine hours, Mother . . . it isn't humanly possible."

I certainly agree.

Farewell on the Mountainside

BETTY BANNER

January 1976

*S*now had fallen all night, and the mountain was a fairy-
land of whiteness. I was twenty-one years old and expecting my first baby in the spring. All my life until the past ten
months had been spent in a fairly good-sized town, and the deep,
narrow valley between the tall mountain and ridge where I was
living with my husband and his mother was a constant source of
interest and new experiences for me. The mountain folks I had
come to know and the many customs of the "old folks" that they
still cherished had formed a new world for me.

During the previous summer I had insisted that we attend the
little white Methodist church about two miles down the valley, and
even though the circuit-rider preacher only came once a month, I
had helped organize a Sunday school for the in-between time.

This particular morning was Monday and "wash day" by an
infallible rule of the mountain community. Snow or no snow, we
washed, and I hummed a gay little tune as I helped my mother-

in-law fill the zinc tubs on the glowing kitchen range and sorted the clothes for washing. My thoughts were of the coming baby, and the warm, steamy kitchen, accentuated by the white coldness seen through the windows, gave me a feeling of security and snugness. While thinking of my own happiness, I talked with my mother-in-law about the pity we felt for a young couple, who, we had been told, had lost their three-week-old baby during the night just the day before. We were still speculating as to what might have caused such a death when a knock at the back door gave us both a start.

Opening the door we were even more startled to see the very same father of the dead child we had just been discussing standing there. His name was John, and he seemed hesitant to come into the kitchen. He just stood twirling his cap in his hands and staring at his feet. All of a sudden he took a deep breath and blurted out, "Betty, we was aimin' to bury our baby today, and now this snow an' all, and the preacher can't get acrost the ridge, and from the way hit's snowin' can't reckon when he could get here." As we started to sympathize, he said, "My Maude . . . she's right smart tore up and ain't able to git outta bed this mornin', but she says we just can't put our baby away 'lessen we have a service over her, and you're the only one I knowed round here I thought could do it."

It was a moment before my stunned brain could take it in that he was talking to and about me. I couldn't believe he was asking me to do the service. I started to stammer that I couldn't possibly preach at a funeral, and besides we couldn't get the car out of the shed even to go two miles down the valley. I might have saved my breath, for he stood there with such grief and stubborn determination in his eyes that I felt like I was butting my head against a brick wall for all the progress I was making.

Then he said quietly, "How'd you feel if it was your young'un?" That did it. I had no answer for that, so I dumbly wiped my still wet hands on my apron and began to untie it. I don't remember another word spoken as I pulled on high rubber boots, coat, and muffler. All I could do was pray frantically over and over, "Dear God, help me. Give me words to help. Help me to say what will comfort them, Lord. . . ."

Leaving word about where I was going for my husband, who was feeding cattle, I set out with John for the long cold walk to the church. Slipping, sliding, often wading through drifts with no conversation between us, the silent white flakes of snow pounded in our faces, until at last we reached the church and went in. My heart came up into my throat. In spite of the snow, the little chapel was filled with mountain folks, and the little homemade coffin rested under a wreath of crepe-paper flowers in front of the rough altar.

It was such a small, crude little chapel, with its oil lamps hanging on the walls, yet in that moment it seemed to me as vast and awesome as St. Patrick's Cathedral, which I once visited. I thought I'd never reach the front, and as I stumbled down the aisle, my frantic brain could only repeat the same prayer. "Dear God, help me, help me. Let me say the words that will help them feel your presence."

When I turned to face the silent congregation, I had to grip the pine pulpit tightly to keep from just going down. It hit me, too, that there was not even a Bible in front of me and I had not thought to bring mine!

As I realized that, I thought, *Well, this is it. I cannot go any further.* And then my eyes fell on that pitiful little box. Then and there God worked a miracle for me, just as surely as if he had reached out and touched my mind and lips. From somewhere unknown, the words came, disjointed as to correctness of quotation I am sure, but essentially those I had heard from early childhood on similar occasions. "I am the resurrection and the life. . . ." "Casting all your care upon Him for He careth for you." "Suffer the children to come unto Me . . . for of such is the kingdom of heaven." On and on the words came, as if a scroll were being unwound before my eyes. Last of all came a prayer—and that was mine, for as I felt my own unborn child stir within me, my petition for a grieving mother in a log cabin on that lonely mountainside found the right words for the final commitment of "earth to earth" at the tiny graveside.

I am now a grandmother, and through the years I have faced many trials and crosses where I have felt like giving up before I started. But always the memory of "my miracle" comes to me, and I go on, for surely the loving God who could give an ignorant twenty-one-year-old girl a funeral service can guide a more mature woman through any difficulty. Always, too, in such a crisis I seem to see John's face and hear the simple words he spoke as I turned from that grave toward home.

"Thank you—I knowed you could do it."

His Mysterious Ways

THAT HOT SUMMER SUNDAY AFTERNOON, my wife and I had been invited to a swimming party at the home of some friends.

With our two children in the care of my grandmother, Cherie and I felt as free as the breeze. As I stood on the diving board, I paused to look up into the serene sky.

Then a frantic voice rose above the party din. At the far end of the pool a woman was screaming. "The baby!" I heard her cry. "He's at the bottom of the pool!"

But no one was doing anything to help. People just stood and stared at her. Confused, I searched the length of the pool and saw what I thought might be a motionless form beneath the water. I dived in—the baby was there. I hurriedly swept him off the bottom and soon laid him on the deck. He'd turned blue . . . no breath. I began CPR.

"Dear God. Help me do it right."

At last the little boy coughed. A short breath came, then another. He would live.

An ambulance was called, for safety's sake. While we waited, I couldn't help asking the others, "Why did you ignore the woman when she said the boy was drowning?"

A friend answered, "None of us understood her, Scott."

"What do you mean? Even at the far end I could hear her yelling about the baby."

"But she's Mexican. None of us understood her Spanish."

"Spanish? I heard her yell in English."

"We didn't. All we heard was Spanish."

"It's true," said the woman's daughter. "Mama can't speak a word of English."

To this day I'm still bewildered. . . . I don't understand a word of Spanish.

—SCOTT BROSTROM, *June 1985*

This Way to Pumpkin Pie

BOB Y.

November 1987

O ne thing we agreed on that crisp fall Sunday was that our supper had to be topped off with fresh, homemade pumpkin pie. It would be the only proper ending for the day.

"Pumpkin pie is nonnegotiable," I laughed, as we drove along a winding country road in the car we'd rented back in New York City. We'd come upstate to see the brilliant colors of the changing foliage, and we'd not been disappointed. Tony, Phil, and I had met several years earlier in an Alcoholics Anonymous group in the city. Back then we were new to AA. Together we'd found sobriety and learned how to ask God for help. From time to time we liked to get together outside AA to share the new direction God was giving our lives.

But on this day our own sense of direction was far from perfect, for during the amiable debate over what, when, and where our old-fashioned country meal would be, we got lost. As the driver, I was being held responsible, and unfortunately the rental car did not come equipped with a New York state road map.

"Maybe God wants to guide us after all," concluded Tony with a chuckle, trying to get me off the hook.

"It's obviously out of your hands," chided Phil, tapping me on the shoulder from the back seat.

Eventually we did come to a little inn. We were ushered to a table in one of the smaller dining rooms, where a fire crackled in the fireplace and paintings of George Washington (who we were assured had slept at this very inn on occasions too numerous to count) adorned the walls. We agreed that this was exactly what we'd had in mind. And they advertised fresh pumpkin pie.

"Something from the bar, gentlemen?" inquired our young waitress. She seemed nervous. Maybe it was her first day on the job, I thought.

"A round of Cokes," Tony said. We nodded our approval. The waitress smiled.

Over appetizers we joked about how important food had become for us in sobriety. "After my first year of not drinking," remarked Phil, "my taste buds grew back. Now whenever I want a drink, I pick up a pizza instead. I just love to eat!"

Our waitress hovered around the table, cleaning ashtrays we had not used and filling our water glasses after nearly every sip. This had to be her first day or something, I thought again.

Finally she left us to devour our dinner of roast duckling and almond chicken, wild rice and fresh, steamed vegetables. No wonder General Washington liked this place.

As soon as our plates were cleared, we were ready for that pumpkin pie. But our waitress shook her head sadly. The last of the lot had just been served.

"We have great apple pie, pecan pie, Indian pudding. . . ."

It was no use. We really wanted pumpkin pie. The way we groaned you would have thought we'd just been informed that pumpkins were suddenly extinct. Without a word, the waitress turned on her heel and left without taking a dessert order. We sat sheepishly stirring our coffee.

"Don't tell anyone," I heard her whisper a few minutes later as she put three pieces of pumpkin pie before us. "The cooks were saving this for themselves, but I talked them out of it. I told them it was important."

"Thanks," I muttered, now rather embarrassed.

"No, thank you," she said, smiling warmly. "You guys don't know what you've done for me today." We looked bewildered, then she came closer. "I'm AA too. I'm new at it and it's been pretty tough. My boyfriend split on me this weekend. I've just been try-ing to hang on. All day I've been praying and praying for strength, and asking God for some sign—anything to tell me everything's going to be all right, that I don't have to pick up a drink. Then out of nowhere, without a reservation or anything, you guys appear, and a table just happens to open up in my section." She paused to catch her breath. "Just when I was feeling lost, you found me. Thanks." And then she was off to another table.

The three of us were silent for a while. There it was again, another example of how God is always there to show us the way when we ask for directions. And sometimes even when we don't.

We cut into our pie. I wasn't surprised to find it was the best pumpkin pie I'd ever tasted.

The Snakebite

DEBBIE DURRANCE

April 1989

We had just finished Sunday dinner when our twelve-year-old son, Mark, asked if he and his dog, Bo, could go out into the field beyond our house for a while. "Just be careful," my husband told him. It was the advice Bobby always gave our children whenever they went out alone, especially in the three years since we'd moved thirty miles out into the brushland of southwestern Florida. Several of our animals had been bitten by rattlesnakes.

As I cleared away the dinner dishes, I watched Mark and Bo race off through the orange and lemon trees of our private oasis. *Mark had become so self-reliant out here in the country,* I thought.

I took my time with the dishes, enjoying the slow Sunday afternoon, and was just finishing up when I heard the living room door open. Suddenly our older son, Buddy, yelled, "Mark, what's wrong?"

I threw down the dish towel and ran toward the living room just as Mark gasped, "I—I've been rattlesnake-bit—" There was a dull thud. When I got there, Mark was on the floor, unconscious. "Go get your dad. Hurry!" I said to Buddy.

I pulled off Mark's shoe; his foot had already swollen into a large, ugly purple mass. There was a musky odor about him, the same odor we'd noticed the times our animals had been bitten by rattlesnakes. In seconds, Bobby rushed in and grabbed Mark up in his arms. "Come on," he said. "We've got to get him to the emergency center."

We ran and climbed into the cab of Bobby's work truck. I held Mark on my lap, Buddy sat in the middle, and Bobby drove. *Oh, God,* I prayed, *help us.* It was seventeen miles to the emergency center, and every minute counted.

Mark was unconscious and convulsions jerked his body. I tried to hold him still, pulling his face close to mine. As long as I could feel his breath against my cheek, I knew he was still alive. But the soft flutters were becoming weaker and less frequent.

"Hurry, Bobby—please hurry!" I pleaded as he frantically passed car after car. Buddy sat in the center, quietly struggling to hold his brother's legs. None of us dared say it, but we all knew we were in a race with death.

As we neared the business section, steam started to seep out from under the hood of the truck. The motor was overheating. About a mile from the clinic, the motor began to pop and sputter.

I glanced over at Bobby. What would we do if the motor stopped? But before I could get the words out, Bobby had to brake for a slower vehicle and the motor cut off completely. I clutched Mark to me, trying to hold on to whatever life was left. We were right in the middle of traffic. Cars were pulling around us and honking their horns. Bobby jumped out and tried to flag down one of the motorists, but the cars just sped around him. "Why won't they stop?" Buddy asked.

Desperate by now, Bobby ran over and pulled Mark from my arms. He carried him out to the rear of the car, where the other drivers could see him, but still the cars kept going by. Finally one old compact car stopped. The driver appeared to be a Haitian farm worker, and he didn't understand English. But he could tell we needed help.

"Thank you, thank you. . ." Bobby shouted as he pulled open the door and pushed Buddy in the backseat. Then he laid Mark down beside him and waved the driver off as I jumped in the front.

"We have to get to the emergency center!" I cried, but his questioning look told me he didn't understand. I pointed in the direction we should go.

As we pulled away, I glanced back at Bobby standing in the street. There was no room for him in the small car and our truck was blocking traffic, but I wished he could be with me.

At the emergency center, medical technicians started working on Mark immediately, trying to stabilize his condition. They started fluids and began artificial respiration. But soon after Bobby arrived, the emergency technicians told us they had done all they could and were transferring Mark to Naples Community Hospital, where Dr. Michael Nycum would meet us.

By the time we arrived at the hospital, Mark had stopped

breathing twice and had gone into a coma. For the next twelve hours, we waited and prayed while the doctors and nurses worked constantly with him. We could tell by the looks on their faces that they didn't expect him to make it.

"Folks, about the only thing the little fellow has going for him is his heart, and that's under tremendous strain," Dr. Nycum told us.

We watched helplessly during the next twenty-four hours as the venom attacked every part of his body. His eyes swelled so tight that all we could see were the ends of his eyelashes. His leg was so swollen the doctors had to make long slashes along it to relieve the pressure on the blood vessels. And still, they were afraid they might have to amputate.

Then, miraculously, Mark passed the crisis point and began to improve a little. He was still in a coma, and certainly not out of danger, but the swelling began to go down.

After that, each day brought improvement. On Thursday, Bobby and I sat there beside Mark's bed. We were drained, exhausted, prayed out. I was sitting in a chair close to him, holding his hand, when I thought I felt a movement. But no, I told myself, it was probably my imagination. A moment later, there it was again, a faint fluttering of the small hand inside mine.

"Bobby," I said, sitting up and reaching across to him. "Bobby! Mark moved—he moved!"

Bobby summoned the nurses and doctor. Mark was coming out of the coma.

"Mom . . . Mom . . ." he moaned.

"Yes, honey, we're here." The words caught in my throat.

"Dad . . ."

"Yes, Son . . ."

His eyes opened now as he looked over at Bobby. "Dad . . . are you mad at me?"

"What do you mean?" Bobby tried to laugh, but it came out a little ragged. "Of course I'm not mad at you."

"I was afraid you'd be mad at me for being so careless."

Bobby reached over and patted Mark on the head. "We're just thankful you're getting better. But what happened, Son? Do you feel like telling us?"

The nurses and Dr. Nycum moved a little closer.

"Well, Bo and I spotted a bird in a cabbage palm and, well, I guess I wasn't paying too much attention to where I was going. I was looking at the bird and jumped over the ditch . . . and my foot landed on something that moved when I hit it.

"And then it was like something slammed down hard on my foot, and my leg started getting real hot. When I looked down, I saw a big rattler had hold of my shoe—it was biting on my foot. It was hurting so bad and Bo was barking and jumping at the snake, but it wouldn't let go. Then Bo jumped on the snake and tore into its head. It let go and crawled off into the bushes.

"Dad, I tried to remember what you said to do if we ever got snakebit, but I was hurting so bad and getting weak and dizzy. I was a long way from the house, and I knew none of you would hear me if I called."

"Where were you, Mark?" Bobby asked.

"Out in the field, a long ways from the house. Out there next to the ditch in the field."

"But that's a third of a mile from the house. How did you get to the house?"

Dr. Nycum shook his head. "Medically speaking, it would have been impossible for him to have walked that far."

Bobby and I looked uncertainly at each other. There were the thirteen steps up to our front door—he'd had to climb those too. I took a deep breath. After everything that had happened, I was almost afraid to ask; but I had to know, "How did you get back to the house, Mark?"

"Well, I remembered you and Dad saying that the more you moved, the quicker the poison would reach your heart, so I knew I couldn't run. But I was so scared, and all I wanted to do was get home. I probably would have run if I could have, but I couldn't because it hurt so bad. And then . . . Dad, there's something I have to tell you. About the man."

"The man? What man?" Bobby asked. "Was someone out there with you?"

"Yes— I mean, no— I mean, I don't know. All I know is that he carried me."

"He carried you?"

"Yes, when I couldn't make it to the house. He picked me up." I could feel a tingle on the back of my neck.

"He talked to me in a real deep voice," Mark went on, "and told me that I was going to be real sick, but that I'd be all right."

"What did he look like?" I asked Mark shakily.

"I couldn't see his face, Mom. All I could see was that he had on a white robe, and his arms were really strong. He reached down and picked me up. And I was hurting so bad, I just sort of leaned my head over on him. He carried me to the house and up the steps. When he put me down, I held on to the door and turned around, and—"

His blue eyes stared into mine with an earnestness I'd never seen before. "All I could see was his back."

For a long time, none of us could speak; it was almost more than we could take in. *God is our refuge and strength,* I said to myself, *a very present help in trouble.*

For most of my life I had believed that passage in the Bible by faith. Now I saw the proof of it.

"Mom . . . Dad . . ." Mark said, hesitating. "I know you may not believe me—"

"We believe you," I whispered as Bobby put his arm around me. "We believe you."

The Unexpected Grandson

NORMA SIMPSON

April 1997

When you're my age, life tends to settle down, without the surprises it once held. At eighty-five, I had grown comfortable with my daily routine in a small lake community in southeast Texas called Toledo Bend. Getting the mail was often a highlight of my day. And that's where I was one summer afternoon a couple years ago—standing at the mailbox—when I opened a red-white-and-blue express-mail envelope and got the shock of my life.

"My name is Tony," the letter read. The writer went on to explain carefully, "I'm your grandson, and I'd like to come to meet you." I turned the envelope over and checked the postmark. *All the way from the East Coast. A far piece to travel for a hoax,* I thought. It just couldn't be true. Could it?

I was thrown back in time to 1955. My only child, Dorothy, single, in her mid-twenties, and living at home, had been crying for days. It just about killed me to see her brilliant blue eyes rimmed with red. Finally she said: "Mother, I'm pregnant."

"Who is the father?" I managed to ask. Dorothy told me. Later I found out he was married. She hadn't known.

Dorothy was a bright girl who graduated from college with a degree in journalism. She had a good job. Her father had died when she was barely out of her teens. We were as close as two people could be. We loved board games and had a closetful of them, passing many an evening intent on our strategies. We liked bird watching, although Dorothy was better at recognizing the rare ones than I was. We laughed like old friends. We were more than mother and daughter; we were a team. And we decided we would raise the baby the way we did most things: together.

Being an unwed mother carried a terrible stigma in our small town. Dorothy and I turned to the church for counseling. During many sessions with our pastor, we discussed what the years had in store for my daughter. We learned about all the couples who were desperate to have a baby but couldn't. Was it right to deprive a child of having two parents? Had we given enough thought to adoption? Gradually it became clear to both of us what was best for the baby. Dorothy went to a maternity home in Cincinnati, where she stayed until her son was born. She cared for him for ten days, then signed the adoption papers—the decision was final and irrevocable.

She returned to me a thin, broken young woman. We never spoke of the baby again. Because Dorothy never mentioned him, neither did I. I would have done anything to spare her further pain.

Eventually she found her calling working as a school librarian, where, she said, "You have the children but don't have to bother with discipline." She went door-to-door electioneering and got herself on the school board so she could do everything in her power to make sure the local kids got the best education possible. I suspected she was trying to fill the void in her life, but of course not even helping every child in the world could have done that. When Dorothy died in my arms from cancer, I felt what she must have felt, that aching sense of loss.

What I didn't know was that while Dorothy was alive, she had spent years seeking information about her son. But the records had been sealed.

Now he's trying to contact me! I thought as I walked slowly up the drive from the mailbox. I put the letter back in the envelope and stuck it in a drawer. *Oh, Dorothy,* I thought, *if you only knew . . .* I didn't sleep well that night, wondering how it is that God works. *Lord, your timing's all wrong,* I thought. How was I to tell if Tony really was who he claimed to be? After all these years, how would I explain him to my friends and family?

Two days later, in the afternoon, a neighbor dropped by for a cup of tea. I was grateful for the diversion. I was trying to keep my mind on our conversation when a forceful knock on the door nearly jolted me out of my seat. *Not now!* I thought. *It can't be him already!* Heart pounding, I opened the door, more intent on the explanation I would give my neighbor than on the tall, trim, dark-haired man in the neat business suit standing there. "Hi," he said softly. "I'm Tony."

Her eyes, her brow . . . I caught myself. "Well, look who's here," I improvised as I motioned him in. "It's Dorothy's . . . friend Tony. He's flown all the way from back East." I smiled at my neighbor, searching her face for signs of suspicion.

"Any friend of Dorothy's is a friend of mine," she said and politely excused herself so we could visit. "Have a nice time, you two." As I let her out, I wondered if I was crazy. Now I was alone with a complete stranger, whether he was my grandson or not. *Lord, please help me handle this.*

"Won't you sit down?" I asked. We chatted for a while before the young man told me his story. When he and his wife decided to have children, he started to look for his birth mother, in part to determine any potential for hereditary medical problems. "But I also wanted to know more about her." With the passage of time and legislation, the records that had been closed to the mother were made available to the son. He had been stunned and saddened to learn Dorothy had died, but heartened to find out about me.

We got comfortable with each other, and then he asked me about Dorothy. No name was sweeter to my ears, no subject dearer to my heart. I began telling him about her, though I did maintain a certain reserve. Finally, saying it was getting late, Tony left for his motel.

When I closed the door I asked myself, *What am I doing? What good could possibly come of this?*

Early the next morning Tony appeared at my door, juggling a pile of luggage. "I'm staying," he announced.

"Who says I want you to?" I shot back with a smile, not completely sure if I was kidding or not. After all, if he were an impostor, he had the perfect scheme to find out anything he wanted to know about me. But again I found myself staring and wondering how many people in this world have Dorothy's brow and eyes.

He squeezed past me and stacked his luggage inside. Tony

had a million questions and asked to see pictures of Dorothy at every age. He read her poems and essays, and letters she had written me. I had saved practically everything, of course. He seemed hungry to know every detail of Dorothy's life. In spite of myself I warmed up to the young man in front of me. I went to bed feeling more comfortable with the situation. *Lord, if this is your will . . .*

The following day I awoke with a start. I grabbed my robe and hustled downstairs. I heard clanking as I approached the kitchen. Tony, wearing the gaudiest pair of gym shorts I had ever seen, was puttering around, making coffee as if he belonged there. "One thing I know about you," I said. "You're colorblind!"

Tony laughed. So did I. We laughed like old friends, and he had me for good. I introduced my grandson to friends, neighbors, relatives, everybody I knew. No one reacted with embarrassment or disapproval. Instead, the people I care about all delighted in my good fortune.

Early that fall Tony arranged for me to fly out to visit him and his wife, who was soon to give birth. We had a fine time. Not long after I returned home, Tony called. "Hey, Great-grandma!" he said, struggling for the words through his emotions. "Say hello to Louisa." I swallowed hard. A baby girl. Louisa, after Dorothy's middle name. Two months later, when Tony flew to Texas with my great-grandbaby, I almost burst with pride at the sight of her.

My health began to deteriorate, and I realized I could no longer live on my own. Tony urged me to come back East with him, but my roots were in Texas. So he returned and set me up in a charming retirement hotel. I never could have managed the move, physically or financially, without him. He takes good care of me now, just as Dorothy would have done. My grandson has enriched my life beyond measure. I had tried to close the door on the past and on the pain of losing a grandson and my beloved Dorothy. But then there came a letter and a knock at the door. . . .

Did I say I was too old for surprises? Not on your life. It's never too late to be surprised by the Lord's blessings.

Author Index

DATE INDEX

NORMAN VINCENT PEALE had a genius for discerning the power in a good idea. When his friend Raymond Thornburg came to him in 1945 with the idea of an inspirational newsletter for businessmen, Dr. Peale sensed immediately that there was an important need to be filled. By that February, the concept had evolved into *Guideposts* magazine.

Guideposts' theme was clear from the single article in that first issue: "I Believe in Prayer" by World War I veteran Captain Eddie Rickenbacker. This magazine would be a place where people from all walks of life—movie stars, business executives, athletes, teachers, housewives, and war heroes—talked about their faith.

The little magazine struggled but subscriptions increased. Then a fire destroyed the magazine's subscriber list. The famous broadcaster Lowell Thomas spoke on his radio show of what had happened to the fledgling publication. The result? *Guideposts* gained even more subscribers than before.

Right from the beginning, readers not only sent in their stories but also their requests for prayer. The staff started to gather regularly on Monday mornings, sharing the requests and praying for readers. The staff also turned to its supporters for inspiration. When financial setbacks threatened to overwhelm the magazine, an early backer accused the staff of thinking *lack*. "Visualize success and you will have it," she said. Positive thinking won the day.

The Young Writers Contest made its appearance in the 1960s, as did the biyearly Writers Workshop. The popular feature "His Mysterious Ways" was inaugurated in 1982. Today the magazine has more pages per issue than ever before, and those prayer requests that used to come by mail now come in the tens of thousands via the Internet. But the purpose of the magazine has never changed.

"Find a need and fill it," was how Dr. Peale would put it. That's been the secret of *Guideposts*' success year after year.